Fundamentals

of

Preventive Maintenance

Fundamentals

of

Preventive

Maintenance

JOHN M. GROSS

AMACOM
American Management Association
New York • Atlanta • Brussels • Buenos Aires • Chicago • London • Mexico City
San Francisco • Shanghai • Tokyo • Toronto • Washington, D.C.

Special discounts on bulk quantities of AMACOM books are available to corporations, professional associations, and other organizations. For details, contact Special Sales Department, AMACOM, a division of American Management Association, 1601 Broadway, New York, NY 10019.
Tel.: 212-903-8316. Fax: 212-903-8083.
Web site: www.amacombooks.org

This publication is designed to provide accurate and authoritative information in regard to the subject matter covered. It is sold with the understanding that the publisher is not engaged in rendering legal, accounting, or other professional service. If legal advice or other expert assistance is required, the services of a competent professional person should be sought.

Library of Congress Cataloging-in-Publication Data

Gross, John M.
    Fundamentals of preventive maintenance / John M. Gross.
       p. cm.
   ISBN 0-8144-0736-6
   1. Plant maintenance.   I. Title.

TS192 .G76 2002
658.2′02—dc21   2002001080

Printing number

10 9 8 7 6 5 4 3 2 1

CONTENTS

Foreword and Acknowledgment   **xi**
> The Best Way to Read This
> Book   xii

Chapter 1   Getting Started   **1**
> Taking Stock of Your
> Situation   1
> Do You Need a Computer to
> Effectively Conduct Daily
> Maintenance and PM
> Activities?   2
> Changing Your Plant's Concept
> of Maintenance and
> Employing Total Productive
> Work   5
> What Are the Magic Steps to
> Implementing the
> Program?   7

Planning for Success   12

Summary   14

Chapter 2 **Establishing Scheduling**   **15**

Why Do I Need to
    Schedule?   15

Establishing the Concept of
    Productive Work   16

How Do I Get Started?   16

What Do I Do with
    Workorders Once They're
    Completed?   30

Do Not Let the Workorder
    Scheduling System Crash and
    Burn   31

Summary   35

Note   36

Chapter 3 **Breaking Your Facility into**
                Logical Parts   **37**

Define "Logical Parts"   38

How Do I Start the
    Process?   41

What Do I Do if I Maintain
    Buildings Instead of
    Plants?   45

Summary   46

Test Time   48

Chapter 4 **Developing an Equipment**
                List   **51**

Creating the Master Equipment
    List's Structure   53

Using Equipment Type   56

Let's Name Everything!   62

Creating the Master List   63

Putting Equipment Numbers
    on Equipment   65

Summary   68

Test Time   69

Chapter 5   Writing PMs   73

Eat the Elephant One Bite at a
    Time   73

Elements of a PM
    Procedure   76

Writing Good
    Instructions   76

Turning the Draft into Final
    PM Workorders   78

Scheduling PMs   80

Quality Assurance of PM
    Write-Ups   81

Summary   83

Test Time   84

**Chapter 6   Developing Equipment
    Manuals   85**

Why Do We Need
    Manuals?   86

How Do We Create These
    Manuals?   87

Where Do We Get the Material
    for These Manuals?   89

What Goes in the Manual
  Under the "Other
  Significant Items"
  Heading?   90
What Are Troubleshooting
  Guides?   91
Reviewing, Editing, and
  Maintaining the
  Manuals   94
Summary   95

Chapter 7   **Setting Up Inventory**   **97**
A Quick Review of Inventory
  Management   98
Inventory Management
  Steps   99
How Do I Add New
  Parts?   114
What About Items That Never
  Get Used?   114
How Will Inventory
  Management Improve
  Uptime?   116
Summary   117

Chapter 8   **Maintaining the System**   **119**
Why Does the World's Greatest
  Maintenance Management
  System Fail?   120
Maintaining Your Quality
  Level   122
Keeping the PM Workorders
  Current   124

What About Parts?   124
Making Continuous
   Improvements (or Like a
   Shark, Move Forward or
   Die)   125
Learning from Your
   Failures   132
More About CMMS
   Programs   134
Summary   135
Test Time   136

Chapter 9   **Planning for Success**   **139**
Who Will Build the PMs and
   the Inventory?   140
What About the Long-Term
   Resources?   142
How Long Will This Take? I'm
   in a Hurry!   143
Summary   148

Chapter 10   **Conclusion**   **151**

Appendix 1   **Abbreviations List**   **153**

Appendix 2   **Generic Equipment List**   **155**

Appendix 3   **PM Procedure Worksheet**   **161**

Appendix 4   **Blank Forms**   **171**
Work Performed Without a
   Workorder   172

Workorder, 8½ × 11
   Basic   173
Workorder, 8½ × 11
   Coordination   174
Workorder, 8½ × 11
   Drawing   175
Workorder, 4 × 8 Size
   (Short Form)   176
Troubleshooting Guide
   Form   177
PM Quality Assurance
   Form   178
Parts Requisition Form,
   8½ × 11 Size   179
Parts Requisition Form, 4 × 8
   Size (Short Form)   180
Daily Shift Log   181
Action Plan   182

Appendix 5   Test Time Answers   **183**

**Appendix 6   Managing the System
              Without a Computerized
              PM Program**   **193**

Appendix 7   Summary of Helpful Tips   **197**

Index   **219**

About the Author   **223**

FOREWORD AND ACKNOWLEDGMENT

I started writing this book as a form of therapy. The book represents the results of my journey of implementing professional maintenance management. I began this journey out of frustration after so many people told me to implement a preventive maintenance (PM) program and a managed inventory, but no one could tell me how! This frustration led me to explore the "how" question and became the basis for this book.

Since that early beginning as therapy, the book has progressed to the point where someone judged it good enough to publish. I wish to thank Neil Levine and his associates at AMACOM books for deeming it as such.

This book would never have been written without the insight and spark from Mr. Trevor Fisk. The encouragement (and prodding) of my wife Karen, however, was the final inspiration to complete the book. Thanks a bunch!

This book also contains numerous illustrations and tips to help clarify its points. I would like to thank the following people for their suggestions and for supplying pictures reproduced in this book: Mr. Ray Harmon, Mr. Greg Luther, Mr. Trevor Fisk, Mr. David Nash, and Mr. Tim Gaffney (John Fabick Tractor Co.).

For those facility people not directly involved in industrial maintenance, you may find the examples to be different from your everyday problems. I hope that the information in this book proves helpful in implementing your own professional maintenance management program.

While the book has an industrial maintenance slant, the necessity for workorder scheduling, a PM program, spare parts, and continuous improvement is universal. The concepts presented will work for your application as well. They will also help you to implement successfully your professional maintenance management program, which includes workorder scheduling, preventive maintenance, and inventory management.

THE BEST WAY TO READ THIS BOOK

To get the most out of this book, I recommend reading it in three passes. On your first pass, flip through the entire book and look at all of the chapters, examining the book's organization and the figures. Get acquainted with the style and flow. On the second pass, go through the book chapter by chapter. At the start of each chapter, conduct another quick review of the chapter. During this review, flip through the chapter looking at the major topics and figures. Finish this review by reading the chapter summary.

On the final pass, go back to the beginning of the chapter and read the entire chapter. During this final pass, look for the detail behind the topics in the chapter summary. Also, make notes and underline important information in the margins.

While this process sounds like it will take forever and slow down your reading, the opposite is true. The three-pass process not only improves comprehension, it also speeds up the reading process.

Now let's get going!

John M. Gross, P.E., C.P.E.

Fundamentals

of

Preventive

Maintenance

GETTING STARTED

✓

*A journey of a thousand miles
begins with the first step.*

TAKING STOCK OF YOUR SITUATION

Does your equipment always breaks down? Do you dream of purchasing new equipment that won't break down? Do you wish you had the resources to develop a full-scale computerized preventive maintenance (PM) program?

Well, you're not alone! Many plant operations people feel their maintenance problems would be over if they had the money for new equipment or for an expensive computer system with support staff. Unfortunately, new equipment is not the answer. Without upfront and continuous PM, new equipment also breaks down. Additionally, without planning and preparation, the most high tech computer system will fail to generate the desired results.

Instead, the answer lies in finding an easy-to-follow and economically feasible approach to PM. The following pages will serve as a roadmap for establishing an effective PM program and improving daily maintenance activities. This approach introduces the concept of "total productive work" that will help you identify unrecognized available resources for developing and conducting the program. If you do not agree with this proposal, then go out and purchase a lottery ticket to use as a bookmark. Once you win the jackpot you can fulfill the dream of new equipment and an expensive computerized PM system.

Do You Need a Computer to Effectively Conduct Daily Maintenance and PM Activities?

The surprising (but true) answer is: It depends! You should base this decision on a number of variables related to your operation. Do you already own (and know how to operate) a computer? Do you have the money to purchase a computer and the necessary maintenance software? Is your operation large enough to warrant a computerized system—for example, do you have one maintenance technician and ten production workers, or do you have fifty maintenance technicians at three different locations? Can you effectively track your inventory without a computerized system? Only *you* can answer these questions.

If you have the resources, need, and desire, then a computerized system will greatly enhance your ability to track scheduled PM activities, costs, workorders, breakdown trends, and repair parts. Additionally, with the advent of low-cost computers and tailored software options, the decision to purchase a computerized system becomes much easier.

However, if you have a large multishift or multilocation operation, then you definitely need a computerized maintenance system. Tracking PM activities, inventory costs, and project workorders, among other things, is a necessity to survive in your world; trying to track them in a large operation without the help of a computerized system would be difficult.

If this situation applies to you and you do not already have a computerized system, aren't looking for a system, or do not think you need a system, then you do not need to read this book. Just put it under your pillow so you can absorb its content by osmosis. Also, be advised that your successor will probably install a computerized system within the first month of your departure.

If you have made the decision to purchase a computerized PM program or computerized maintenance management system (CMMS), then you need to select a program that meets your needs. Don't let the information technology (IT) group make the decision for you. Instead, to assess whether the system will help manage your operation and not force you to change to fit the program, use the selection criteria outlined in Figure 1-1.

Regardless of your decision, most effective PM programs start out on paper. As a matter of fact, in the "old

Figure 1-1. Questions to ask when selecting a computerized PM program.

____ Does the program's data-handling structure parallel how you want to organize your PM program?

____ Does the program allow you to create naming structures that have meaning to you (and your associates)?

____ Does the program generate reports in your desired format?

    ❑ If not, will the vendor customize the program to meet your needs at a reasonable fee?

____ Does the program have the potential to grow along with your business? (Remember, spending a few extra bucks now can avoid a mountain of nightmares and cost later!) For example:

    ❑ Can the program accommodate handheld computers or personal data assistants (PDAs)? (Do not dismiss this requirement—handheld devices may become the biggest administrative time-saver since the PC.)

    ❑ Can the program be hosted on a local area network (LAN) or a wide area network (WAN)?

____ Can you manipulate the data files with mainstream database programs such as dBASE, Access, or Paradox? Will the vendor provide instructions on converting to and from these formats?

    ❑ A "no" answer to either question should signal a "no" buying decision.

❑ If the vendor answers "yes" to the second
   question, be sure to have conversion
   specifications included in the purchase order or
   quote.

___ Does the program handle sorting, naming, and
    cataloging of repair parts in a way that fits your
    operation and planned inventory organizational
    scheme?

___ How much data entry and upkeep will the program
    require?

❑ Who will keep the data in the system updated?

---

days" most PM programs existed as card files that tracked
and scheduled equipment workorders and PMs (it should
also be noted that these card systems required clerical
support and a lot of tribal knowledge to operate). If you
choose not to purchase a computerized PM program, see
Appendix 6 for details on how to manage this system
manually without the aid of a computerized program.

CHANGING YOUR PLANT'S CONCEPT OF MAINTENANCE AND EMPLOYING TOTAL PRODUCTIVE WORK

As part of the process of developing an effective PM program, you also need to change your mind-set (and those
of your employees) about maintenance. Many plant
managers and maintenance managers have heard this

canned phase from their mechanics: "If we're not busy, then it must be running!" This statement is usually accompanied by an all-knowing, nonverbal facial expression that says, "Relax, we're taking care of you, so leave us alone."

Well, they are wrong (and so are you if you leave them alone). To survive in today's world of "lean and mean" operations, you cannot wait for breakdowns. As a matter of fact, you should make responding to breakdowns or troublecalls the exception in your daily workload. A successful and effective maintenance operation has to break away from the "fix it when it breaks" mentality. The successful operation does not reward heroic repairs, but rather looks at the catastrophic breakdowns, which require heroic repairs, as failures of the PM program. These occurrences should be viewed as items for follow-up and correction. The success of the maintenance operation must be measured in uptime and not how many breakdowns get repaired. Finally, PM instructions (PMs) or repairs should be made before equipment breaks down. This philosophy has the added advantage of allowing you to schedule the work rather than letting the work schedule you.

So if mechanics do not run around all day going from one breakdown to the next, then what do they do all day? They perform workorders: PMs, correctives, or projects. They are working on assigned workorders and responding to troublecalls as needed. If production has a high-priority piece of equipment that requires babysitting, then issue the assigned mechanic simple workorders that allow quick and immediate response to equipment problems. Employ the concept of total productive work (TPW)—schedule your maintenance activities to maximize the productivity of your crew.

Rather than thinking "if we're not busy, it must be running," the new mind-set now becomes: "If the crew's not busy, then they are not being productive (and I have not scheduled their time properly)!" When you begin to schedule your maintenance activities, you will be amazed at how much more you get accomplished. As a matter of fact, effective scheduling will show you where to get the resources to develop and execute your PM program.

One final note about this new mind-set: When you introduce the concept of total productive work, don't expect all of your employees to dance in the aisles and immediately begin building your shrine. People are resistant to change. As you begin scheduling your crew's time, they will realize it's not business as usual. Be aware of potential negative perceptions of this new culture and work with your crew to help them understand why the new mind-set is vital to the company's continued success.

Additionally, as you become aware of individuals who do not pull their weight, do not shy away from the issue—let them know you're not satisfied with their performance and expect improvement.

WHAT ARE THE MAGIC STEPS TO IMPLEMENTING THE PROGRAM?

I've said it once and I'll say it again—there is no magic formula for implementing professional maintenance management! The process takes time and commitment to succeed. Therefore, instead of a magical quick fix, this book instead proposes a seven-step process (see Figure 1-2) for achieving the goal of professional maintenance management. I'll outline these steps in the following paragraphs and then elaborate on each step in greater detail in subsequent chapters.

STEP 1: ESTABLISH SCHEDULING

Establish a scheduling process to plan out the daily activities of the maintenance staff. This process will consist of setting up a filing system that contains files for 1) each shift over a thirty-one-day period and 2) each month of the year. You then use this system to schedule your workorders by day and by shift. The scheduling process will allow you to take control of daily activities. This step also gives you a means to begin scheduling the activities required to set up a PM program. Of all the steps in-

Figure 1-2. Seven basic steps to professional maintenance management.

1. Establish scheduling.

2. Break down the facilities into logical parts.

3. Develop an equipment list and assign equipment numbers.

4. Develop and issue preventive maintenance (PM) instructions.

5. Locate and/or develop equipment manuals.

6. Develop a managed inventory.

7. Monitor the program's effectiveness and make improvements.

volved in establishing professional maintenance management, scheduling can be the toughest, but it is the most critical. Without successful scheduling you cannot hope to meet all your maintenance commitments—trouble-calls, correctives, and PMs.

STEP 2: BREAK DOWN THE FACILITIES INTO LOGICAL PARTS

Develop a map of each of your facilities that breaks the building up into logical parts. Breaking up the plant sets the stage for record-keeping activities and creates a framework for scheduling the PM workorder instruction-writing process. Use the facility's physical structure, production processes, product lines, and cost centers to define what is "logical" for your program. No matter how you decide to break up the facility, make the structure meaningful to you and your staff. Incidentally, this step is the perfect opportunity to start getting people on board for the rest of the process. Having your staff participate in the mapping process allows them to develop ownership of the program.

Don't overcomplicate this process—you are not inventing the replacement for the Dewey decimal system. Develop a simple easy-to-follow breakdown that everyone can understand and use. This is especially important if you plan *not* to do all the maintenance by yourself. (By the way, if you plan to build the PM program by yourself, then you either have a very small plant or you've missed the boat on how to successfully develop and conduct a successful maintenance management program.)

STEP 3: DEVELOP AN EQUIPMENT LIST AND ASSIGN NUMBERS

Once you've completed the facility map, then identify and number all the pieces of equipment in the facility.

This list will serve as the structure for tracking equipment maintenance activities. During this phase you will need to develop a numbering system for the orderly assignment of equipment numbers. Appendix 1 has a suggested generic numbering system that can serve as a starting point for your tailored system. You will accomplish this step by issuing workorders to gather data (e.g., S/N, model, size, manufacturer, age) on each piece of equipment in the newly mapped areas. With this data, you can then assign numbers to each piece of equipment.

Once again the caution flag goes out: Don't overcomplicate the numbering system. The numbers are meant to track workorder transactions; this isn't to be a code-breaking exercise. Be leery of developing a numbering system that has fifteen digits (with each digit having a special meaning). Instead, consider the simple six- or seven-digit numbering scheme proposed in Appendix 2.

Step 4: Develop and Issue Preventive Maintenance Instructions (PMs)

In this step, you will develop PM workorder instructions for all the pieces of equipment identified in the previous step. The PM workorders should include all necessary activities for each interval (e.g., weekly, monthly, quarterly). Your existing equipment manuals and the writer's individual experience will serve as the source of information for these initial PMs. Appendix 3 contains a PM Procedure Worksheet that can help in development of the initial PM workorders.

Writing the work instructions is only half the battle; you also need to send them out for a trial run. You will find out about their appropriateness, completeness, and usefulness after issuing the PMs several times. During the early phases, you will also learn how to schedule these workorders. Expect some resistance to change. Be ready for and open to feedback. Use this feedback to help improve your program. Also realize that these initial PM workorders will be the first of several versions. Over time events will occur (e.g., breakdowns, addition of new technology, new people's experiences, or vendor recommendations) that will highlight areas for improvement.

Step 5: Locate and/or Develop Equipment Manuals
This step develops the troubleshooting information that rounds out the successful maintenance organization. Most maintenance shops have "manuals," but it is the quality of these manuals that really matters. A good manual addresses operating procedures, troubleshooting guides, schematics, PLC programs (if applicable), parts lists, and other items (such as manuals for specific process control equipment).

Step 6: Develop a Managed Inventory
This step focuses on creating a managed inventory that contains the parts necessary to minimize downtime without duplicating the national debt. A managed inventory will track the ins and outs of repair parts and generate reorder reports. The system will also allow you to track repair history and cost. You will need a plan for where to put parts, how to store parts, what parts to remove, what parts to add, and how to maintain the inventory.

During this step, it pays to get your vendors involved in planning, organizing, and setting up of the inventory. After all, parts are their business! Vendors can also conduct equipment surveys to help determine what items should be stocked in the parts inventory. If wisely used, your vendors will be an incredible resource for creating this inventory and for setting up a competitive-pricing structure.

Step 7: Monitor the Program's Effectiveness and Make Improvements

Like all successful programs, the PM program and the inventory won't run by themselves. Your success depends on continued commitment and management. Additionally, as you administer the program, you will need to modify items that do not work or were overlooked.

As simple as this step sounds, lack of commitment sinks more PM programs than any other factor. Coincidentally, lack of long-term commitment also impedes the success of even the most simple workorder programs. Translation: While it's easy to fill out those little pieces of paper, it's harder than hell to track and to complete workorders if they are not managed. It becomes very easy to "cancel" the PM workorders because of other, "more important" priorities.

The downward spiral for your inventory occurs the same way. You stop checking out parts, so the reorder reports become ineffective. Now without the reorder reports, you order what you "think" you need and you subsequently return to inventory firefighting.

PLANNING FOR SUCCESS

Chapter 9 of this book addresses developing an implementation program. I suggest you read Chapters 2 through 8 carefully to become familiar with the concepts and resource requirements for developing a maintenance management system before embarking on implementation. Some chapters contain practical exercises to help reinforce that chapter's concepts. These exercises, titled "Test Time," are placed after the chapter summary and the answers are contained in Appendix 5. I recommend you try these exercises as another method for reinforcing the seven-step program development process. Once you have read the other chapters, then use the tips in Chapter 9 to prepare an implementation roadmap or plan. The roadmap will formalize how you plan to implement the seven-step program and resources required. By formalizing your plan, you force yourself to think through the steps and you create a vehicle for coordination of your plan. You cannot implement this program in a vacuum, so the process of upfront coordination ensures that everyone (e.g., your crew and your management) knows the plan and the timeline. The coordination process also creates an opportunity to receive advice and feedback on how to improve the plan.

As you read the following chapters, consider what resources you have that can help in completion of each task. Unless you have a very small operation, you will not be able to develop a PM program and a managed inventory by yourself. As you read this book, begin preparing to develop a team to implement the tasks in this book. As a side benefit, you'll find that implementation of the PM program and managed inventory can be a vehicle for creating or improving teamwork within your group.

You should also consider any additional resources you will need to implement and maintain this program. Consider how you can redirect assignments to fill these needs if adding staff is not an option.

Summary

The proposed process allows you to build the program one step at a time. The early steps will allow you to see immediate improvements while still completing the rest of the program. The process of implementing a PM program and creating a managed inventory will not be easy, but the reward will be worth the effort. If you're still interested in implementing professional maintenance management, then read on!

2

ESTABLISHING SCHEDULING

✓

*One for the money, two for the
show, three to get ready, and
four to . . .*

WHY DO I NEED TO SCHEDULE?

Why do I need to schedule my guys—we're too
small, my guys know what they need to do, and
I'm too busy! These are just a few of the reasons that
people give for not planning and scheduling. They also
sow the seeds for equipment failures, late-night calls, dis-
trustful production people, and irate bosses. Instead,
maintenance managers should view scheduling as the
cornerstone of successful maintenance operations.

Scheduling involves planning the activities of the
maintenance crew. It does not mean planning the minute-

by-minute schedule of each technician. Planning means assigning workorders by shift, by day, by task importance, by material availability, by manpower availability, and by production downtime.

ESTABLISHING THE CONCEPT OF PRODUCTIVE WORK

This book centers on the concept of total productive work (TPW)—or maximizing the productive activities of the maintenance team through proactive professional maintenance management. Total productive work means scheduling your crew to handle the daily troublecalls while maximizing the number of completed workorders. You eliminate mechanics standing around waiting for breakdowns because they are busy with workorders. TPW also allows you to plan for those daily problems that seem to pop up.

Once you accept that you have only so many resources available for all the activities you would like to get done, then scheduling becomes very appealing. Scheduling lets you plan for the daily troublecalls while still completing workorders.

HOW DO I GET STARTED?

First, if you don't have workorders, then you need to get some. Appendix 4 shows several examples of workorders that I have used. If you don't like these sample forms, then create your own workorder forms or check if your local printer has examples. To create your own form, simply use the format options available on most spreadsheet or word processing programs to develop a form that meets your needs.

Once you find a form that suits you, then make copies and distribute. Copies should, however, only be a short-term fix. To create a professional-looking form, have a printer make a two-part carbonless form. With a two-part form, you get the original and the originator (or author) of the workorder can keep a copy.

If you already have workorders (or once you have created them), then follow the steps in Figure 2-1 to establish a scheduling system. These steps will create a structure for scheduling workorders and allow you to identify how much available time you have for completing workorders. Throughout this chapter, Helpful Tips have been included to guide you through the rough spots that can slow down or stop the program.

SET UP SHIFT FILES

The first step toward setting up scheduling is to set up files that allow you to organize the workorders for each

Figure 2-1. Steps for establishing scheduling.

1.	Set up shift files.
2.	Calculate available scheduling hours.
3.	Sort the workorders by priority.
4.	Develop a schedule by day and by shift.
5.	Keep scheduling.

shift. To set up the files, purchase 105 folders (simple letter-size manila folders will do just fine) and label them as follows:

◆ Label a folder for each day of the month and shift. For example:

Label	Meaning
1-1	First shift on the first of the month
1-2	Second shift on the first of the month
1-3	Third shift on the first of the month

◆ Label the rest of the folders the same way for the remaining thirty-one days of the month (e.g., 2-1, 2-2, 2-3 . . . 31-1, 31-2, and 31-3).

◆ Label the last twelve folders for the months of the year for those workorders that you cannot do immediately, but will do later.

You now have a rotating set of scheduling folders for organizing and storing your daily workorders. Once you start scheduling, then your supervisor or team leader simply goes to the files, pulls the appropriate file folder (by day and by shift), and distributes the assigned workorders.

CALCULATE AVAILABLE SCHEDULING HOURS

If you want to truly schedule your people, then you need to know how many hours you have available for scheduling on each shift. To figure available hours, first calculate how many total hours exist on each shift. To calculate the total available hours, use this formula:

```
Total available work hours = (Number of
technicians × Number of hours/shift) −
Time for breaks and lunches
```

Next, estimate how much time your technicians devote to troublecalls. Once you have this number, then subtract it from the total available work hours to calculate the total available time for scheduling preventive maintenance instructions (PMs) and projects. The formula is:

```
Total available time for scheduling =
Total available work hours − Time for
troublecalls
```

For example, if you have a ten-person crew working eight hours a day, and each person gets two ten-minute breaks and thirty minutes for lunch and devotes half their time to troublecalls, then you have 31.7 hours/day available for scheduling. Figure 2-2 shows the detailed calculation for arriving at this number.

What is the benefit of making these calculations? First, by calculating the total available time, you'll realize just how much time you really have to get things done. It also highlights how much time your crew devotes to answering troublecalls (i.e., fighting fires). Once armed with this information, you can start to sort through the pile (or piles) of open workorders and begin to determine how and when you can schedule them.

SORT THE WORKORDERS BY PRIORITY

In the beginning, simply take your open workorders and begin sorting them by level of importance. If you do not already have a set of priorities in mind, then use these:

1 Safety hazards
2 Repairs affecting safety
3 Repairs affecting operations
4 Preventive maintenance
5 Projects

As you sort the workorders, assign an estimate of the time and the number of people required to complete the

Figure 2-2. Calculating total time available.

Givens:

Crew Size	= 10 people
Number of Hours/Shift	= 8 hours
Number of Length of Breaks	= 2 breaks, 10 minutes each
Length of Lunch Break	= 30 minutes
Estimated Time Spent on Troublecalls	= 4 hours/person (or half of the shift)

Calculation:

Total Available Work Hours	= Total Work Hours − Time for Breaks and Lunches
Total Work Hours	= 10 people × 8 hours/shift
	= 80 hours
Time for Breaks and Lunches	= 10 people × (2 × 10 minutes) + 10 people × 30 minutes
	= 500 minutes/shift
	= 500/60 minutes/hour
	= 8.3 hours/shift
Total Available Work Hours	= 80 hours − 8.3 hours
	= 71.7 hours
Total Available Time for Scheduling	= Total Available Work Hours − Time for Troublecalls
Time for Troublecalls	= 10 people × 4 hours/shift
	= 40 hours/shift
Total Available Time for Scheduling	= 71.7 hours/shift − 40 hours/shift
	= 31.7 hours/shift

requested work. You will need this information later when determining where the workorder fits in the schedule. At this point, don't get hung up on trying to assign numbers with deadly accuracy. Instead, focus on getting the workorders sorted so you can get started scheduling.

DEVELOP A SCHEDULE BY DAY AND BY SHIFT

Once you have completed the sorting, then the fun of scheduling all those workorders starts! As complicated as some people want to make scheduling, it boils down to simply figuring out where everything fits within the constraints of time, people, and materials. To help this process, use decision rules, such as those listed in Figure 2-3, for scheduling.

Before beginning the scheduling process, always think about how many available hours exists on any given shift. When you schedule, match the amount of scheduled work to the available hours. If you put a bunch of workorders in the file without determining how many work-

Figure 2-3. Suggested decision rules for scheduling.

1. Where do you have available hours (i.e., manpower)?

2. Is this workorder urgent (e.g., a safety hazard or an impending equipment failure)?

3. When will the equipment be available?

4. Which shift has the necessary skills to perform the work?

5. When will all the parts be available?

orders can actually be completed, you risk creating a smorgasbord mentality among the members of the crews. When this happens, your technicians will pick the workorders they want to complete. (Be advised that their choices may not match your needs or desires.)

Another obstacle to avoid is scheduling all your number-one priorities in the first week. Mix and match small priorities with the big ones. If all the scheduled workorders have top priority, then you severely limit your flexibility and ability to adapt the workorder schedule for the crisis that always seems to occur. Take a long-range view of scheduling and make use of all of those new folders to spread out the workorders. You will be amazed how much more manageable the workorder pile becomes when you spread them out over all the shifts in a one-month period.

HELPFUL TIP 1

If you get a workorder you do not know how to complete (but it sounds like a good idea), then schedule it as a two-part workorder.

Part 1   Planning

Part 2   Execution

This technique keeps the workorders moving and does not make you personally responsible for developing every repair solution. This approach also starts the empowerment process by forcing your mechanics to start thinking about how to fix the plant's problems.

The final step in setting up your scheduling system is to decide if you want to schedule the workorders by shift or by specific people on the shift. The main factor in making this decision should be the type of leadership you have on each shift. The best situation is to assign the workorders by shift—letting each shift decide who gets which workorders. This approach makes each shift part of the process. Scheduling by shift also makes your schedule less dependent on the right people being at the right place at the right time.

KEEP SCHEDULING

Once you begin to schedule your crew's work, then you need to *just keep doing it!* The Helpful Tips offered throughout this chapter will make the job easier.

HELPFUL TIP 2

Set up a two-week scheduling board that allows you to plan where and when you perform the workorders. The board's objective is to create a visual management tool to use in planning your daily and weekly schedule. Setting up a scheduling board is simple:

◆ Buy a "dry erase board" from a local office supply store.

◆ Buy pinstriping from a local auto supply store.

◆ Using the pinstripes, mark off grids for each shift covering fourteen days.

The scheduling board allows you to work through "what if" situations while preparing a weekly schedule. You will find scheduling is not so overwhelming when you can move the workorders around on the board and see what happens to the schedule if the work is moved up a day or two or pushed back a week. Once you have decided on the schedule, you have a visual record of the plan for your review. The completed board will also help in dealing with all those people who want to know when their workorder is scheduled.

Figure 2-4 is an example of a scheduling board where the maintenance manager has chosen to set up the schedule on half of the board and leave the rest for notes. The number of boards used will vary by the size of the organization, but typically most organizations use one to two boards that are 3 × 5 or 4 × 8. I worked with a large organization that used two boards, each measuring four-feet by eight-feet, for scheduling.

HELPFUL TIP 3

If you experience a large percentage of troublecalls, assign specific technicians on a rotating basis to respond to

Figure 2-4. An example of a scheduling board.

them. Give the float technician small, low-priority work-orders to complete between calls. This tactic lets you keep fighting the fires and still get some PM and project work-orders done. (Remember: If you want to get out of the firefighting mode, then PMs and projects are key.)

Use the form for Work Performed Without a Work-order, shown in Figure 2-5, to keep track of the trouble-calls rather than forcing everyone to write a million after-the-fact workorders. (Appendix 4 contains a blank copy of this same form for your use.) Technicians fill out one of the blocks on this form when they respond to a troublecall. Someone then enters these forms into your computerized maintenance management system (CMMS) program as completed workorders.

If you use this form, then tailor its format to be compatible with your CMMS workorder entry screen.

HELPFUL TIP 4

Set up workorder bins to hold parts for scheduled work-orders. Number the bins and write the appropriate bin number on the scheduled workorder. By putting parts in the bins, you eliminate the need for technicians to hunt for the parts required to complete a workorder. The bins help you keep track of incoming project or repair parts and you create a place to store parts required for ongoing long-term projects.

HELPFUL TIP 5

Create a filing system for workorders placed on hold while awaiting parts. This "system" can be as simple as a clipboard with the workorders and copies of the purchase orders stapled together. The workorder comes off the clip-

Figure 2-5. Work performed without a workorder.

WORK PERFORMED WITHOUT A WORKORDER

BE SURE YOU RECORD DOWNTIME FOR MACHINE
DEPT#_____ EQPT#_____ LABOR HRS_____ MACH DOWNTIME_____ DATE_____	TECHNICIAN:_____ EMP #_____ EQUIPMENT DESCRIPTION:_____ PROBLEM:_____ _____ ACTION:_____

Make sure you capture this information.

Write down a simple description of the problem and the corrective action.

BE SURE YOU RECORD DOWNTIME FOR MACHINE
DEPT#_____ EQPT#_____ LABOR HRS_____ MACH DOWNTIME_____ DATE_____	TECHNICIAN:_____ EMP #_____ EQUIPMENT DESCRIPTION:_____ PROBLEM:_____ _____ ACTION:_____

A technician fills in a block every time he responds to a troublecall.
- Collecting this data will allow collection of trend data on individual equipment pieces and equipment groups.
- Using this form also avoids the problem of chasing after-the-fact workorders.

BE SURE YOU RECORD D(
DEPT#_____ EQPT#_____ LABOR HRS_____ MACH DOWNTIME_____ DATE_____	TECHNICIAN:_____ EQUIPMENT DESCRIPTI(PROBLEM:_____ _____ ACTION:_____

BE SURE YOU RECORD DOWNTIME FOR MACHINE
DEPT#_____ EQPT#_____ LABOR HRS_____ MACH DOWNTIME_____ DATE_____	TECHNICIAN:_____ EMP #_____ EQUIPMENT DESCRIPTION:_____ PROBLEM:_____ _____ ACTION:_____

board when you receive the parts and they have been placed in a workorder bin.

HELPFUL TIP 6

Allow your technicians to fill out purchase requests for your review and approval. Allowing technicians to identify the required parts not only prevents you from becoming a bottleneck, but improves their knowledge.

HELPFUL TIP 7

Cross-reference your workorders and purchase requests to reduce confusion. Cross-referencing ensures that incoming parts get used for their original purpose. The cross-referencing process works like this:

◆ Write the workorder number on the purchase request.

◆ Write the purchase request number on the workorder.

◆ Have the workorder number listed on the address header of the shipping receipt.

◆ File the workorder in the system created in Helpful Tip 5 and wait for the part to arrive.

If you use the cross-reference, when a part arrives, the workorder number is right in front of you on the purchase order. You can now use the information on the shipping receipt to identify the intended use of the part.

HELPFUL TIP 8

Forward-schedule the weekend (or plant shutdown) workorders. To forward-schedule, put workorders that require downtime in the day shift folder of the next nonwork day (e.g., Saturday, Christmas, or whenever). By forward scheduling, you can forecast the workload for these days. Additionally, you get the workorders off your desk and into a place where they will not be lost. As the holiday or nonwork day approaches, pull the file and schedule the workorders.

HELPFUL TIP 9

Develop a summary sheet to track the scheduled workorders for each shift. This summary sheet should list the scheduled workorders and the names of the technicians scheduled for that shift. Figure 2-6 is an example of a daily shift log. Place this sheet in each schedule folder once you complete the schedule. By reviewing this sheet on the following day, you'll know at a glance what you scheduled and how it matches against what really hap-

Figure 2-6. Daily shift log used to track the scheduled workorders.

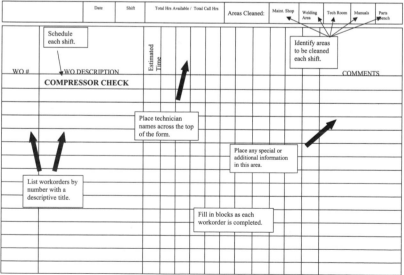

pened. Likewise, you'll know if a workorder does not come back. (Appendix 4 contains a blank copy of a daily shift log for your use.)

Do not let technicians hold on to workorders. By requiring technicians to return all workorders to the schedule folder at the end of the shift, you prevent lost workorders and you can track the shift's accomplishments.

HELPFUL TIP 10

Coordinate your schedule with the production folks. Yes—I mean talk to the production scheduler, supervisor, or manager to make sure your plan does not conflict with their plan. In the best-case scenario, you can develop a schedule that meets both of your needs. In the worst-case scenario, you will avoid the frustration (and possible pain) of having production short-circuit your perfectly planned schedule.

HELPFUL TIP 11

If deciding on priorities becomes a nerve-racking experience, then use the prioritization system proposed by Alec Mackenzie in his book *The Time Trap*.[1] In his book, Mackenzie recommends ranking tasks by long-term importance and short-range urgency. To use this method, look at each task and give the task a rank (e.g., 1–3) for importance and urgency. Next, add up both scores and then schedule the lowest numbers. There is one exception: Do all the safety hazard workorders immediately.

If time management is a personal productivity issue, then I recommend reading *The Time Trap*. This book will help you improve your time management skills by identifying personal time-wasters and by helping to develop a personal improvement plan.

WHAT DO I DO WITH WORKORDERS ONCE THEY'RE COMPLETED?

Like some of life's other activities, the job's not done until the paperwork is complete. When the workorders come back completed in the daily files, then close them out. Closing them out can mean closing the workorder in the computer or sending the workorder out for sign-off by the originator in a manual system.

If you have a computerized system, then (for PM workorders) update the appropriate file on the system and throw away the workorder. Yes—throw away the workorder. Your computer program files will serve as the historical record. These files will also satisfy management system audits for ISO-9000 quality system programs or the automotive industry's QS-9000.

For project or corrective workorders, close the work-order out on the computer and send the workorder to the originator for sign-off. The originator should only return the workorder if there's disagreement with the closure actions.

By not holding on to the old workorders, you free filing space and avoid duplication. You also save the time required to file the paperwork.

In a manual system, create a separate file folder for each piece of equipment on the factory equipment list. (You'll learn how to develop this list in Chapter 4.) These folders will serve as the historical record of all your main-tenance activities. As workorders get completed, then they should be filed in the appropriate file folder. You now have the supporting documentation to track trends and to show proof of workorder activities.

For project workorders, send the completed workorder to the originator for acceptance of the work. When they return the signed workorder, then file the workorder in the appropriate file folder.

For a large factory, the size of the files and the upkeep requirements will be huge. The amount of effort required to successfully complete this activity serves as another justification for a computerized PM program.

HELPFUL TIP 12

When reviewing potential computerized PM programs, ask the vendor to show you how the program handles opening and closing workorders. A cumbersome system can tie up a lot of administrative time in trying to manage the workorders. A cumbersome system can also prevent you from using the full power of the program. When this situation occurs you will eventually stop entering the workorders until they are complete. When selecting an automated program:

- ◆ **Be sensitive to the number of screens needed to open and close workorders.**

- ◆ **Check if the program allows you to close the workorders from a single menu screen.**

DO NOT LET THE WORKORDER SCHEDULING SYSTEM CRASH AND BURN

What could possibly go wrong with such a well-thought-out and logical scheduling system? Answer: You stop managing all those little pieces of paper called workorders! If you do not continually track and keep the workorders moving through the system, then they become another millstone around your neck.

To keep the system operating, use the flow we've created in this chapter. This process (shown in Figure 2-7) allows you to keep up the workorder flow, which is key to the success of scheduling. Also, use the following steps on a daily basis to prevent a fatal crash of your workorder scheduling system:

◆ Review the shift files from the previous day and take care of the workorders—close them out, reschedule them to another shift, or put them on hold for parts, planning, or coordination.

◆ Use the shift summary sheet (see Helpful Tip 9) to track the workorders sent out.

◆ Ask what happened if all the planned workorders did not get completed. Was there an emergency breakdown? Were there production problems, or just too many coffee breaks or people working on their own pet projects, etc.?

◆ Check the filing system created in Helpful Tip 5 to track the on-hold workorders. As part of this check, identify and follow up on those workorders with past-due dates for parts.

◆ Do not create "special" workorder piles on your desk.

◆ Forward-schedule workorders. For example, if an incomplete workorder comes back on Tuesday, but you know you cannot get back to it until Thursday afternoon, then immediately put that workorder in the Thursday afternoon file.

Figure 2-7. Workorder scheduling flow.

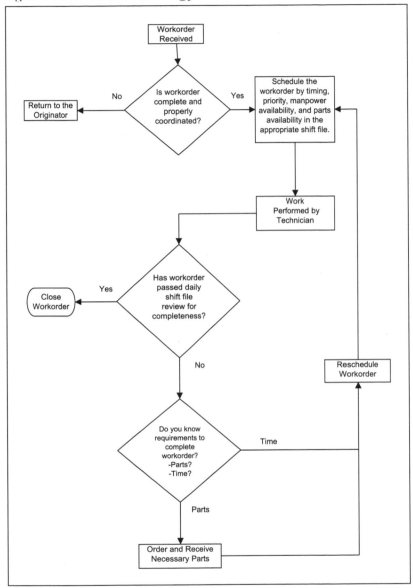

Also, avoid becoming the plant's maintenance secretary. If someone wants something done, then hand them a workorder.

I once visited a plant that had this problem. During my opening meeting I discovered that managers didn't use workorders, did not schedule, and never did preventive maintenance—they just fought fires all the time. My first recommendation—start a workorder scheduling system. Upon further discussion about workorders, I discovered they *had* used workorders and they even had a box containing 1,000 workorders. When I asked the maintenance manager what happened, he stated that the plant stopped using workorders because no one would fill them out or they (the production folks) always wanted him to fill them out. With this type of response, you do not have to be a brain surgeon to figure out why they were always fighting fires. Don't fall into this rut. Make everyone responsible for writing their own workorders!

Finally, do not be afraid to reject workorders. Just because someone has a pen and can write doesn't mean all their ideas, wants, or desires should be implemented. If a workorder does not make sense, then send it back. If you receive a workorder that has not been coordinated, then send it back. If you do not think you have the authority to execute a particular workorder, then send the workorder to the appropriate level. Rejecting workorders will not create problems if you follow one rule: Tell the originator why you sent it back!

It's never acceptable to reject a workorder just because "It's the dumbest idea I've ever heard," or "We do not allow line workers to write workorders." It is, however, *acceptable* to reject a workorder if:

◆ It is unsafe.

◆ It will create quality problems.

◆ It has not been coordinated properly.

Most of the workorders I have "kicked back" in my career were for lack of coordination. Save yourself a boatload of problems and make the workorder's authors do their own coordination when you encounter this situation. Do not put yourself in the position of explaining why you did something that everybody else hates. (When this situation arises, you will probably find out that you now *own* this *great idea* and will receive all of the heat. Congratulations!)

SUMMARY

If you do not implement any other recommendations in this book except the ones in this chapter, then you are already money ahead. Scheduling the maintenance crew's daily work will let you set the department's agenda and squeeze out those extra drops of productivity.

To implement scheduling, set up the shift files, calculate available hours, sort through the current backlog, and schedule these workorders based on priorities and available resources. On a daily basis, review the previous day's shift files, process the workorders, and finalize the next day's schedule. Review the Helpful Tips for suggestions on how to improve your scheduling activities. Finally, do not fall into the traps of being the plant's maintenance secretary or workorder coordinator.

Also, always remember that not all workorders were

meant for execution (thank goodness). However, when you reject workorders, always provide a reason, such as decreased safety, lack of coordination, or reduced quality.

If you have made the decision to schedule workorders, then remember this process will take time for you to master. In the initial phases of scheduling, you may even make one or two little (or big) mistakes. Welcome to the real world. Learn from these mistakes and keep on scheduling!

NOTE

1. Alec Mackenzie, *The Time Trap: The Classic Book on Time Management,* 3rd edition (New York: AMACOM, 1997), pp. 38–39.

BREAKING YOUR FACILITY
INTO LOGICAL PARTS

✓

Dad, can we write PMs yet?

Now that everyone has started scheduling, it's time to begin working on a PM program. However, before we begin the actual process of writing PM instructions, we need to break down the facility into logical parts and create a structure for the plant's equipment list. By breaking the plant into parts, you set the stage for follow-on record-keeping activities and create a framework for scheduling the writing of PM work instructions. Additionally, computerized PM programs will require some type of structure to serve as the framework for managing assets.

This step also provides an upfront opportunity to introduce people to the PM development process. If you do not get your associates to take ownership of the PM system, then you have a high probability of failure. Don't miss any opportunity to get your folks involved!

Define "Logical Parts"

How do you decide on what "logical" means? The answer is simple: It's any division of the plant that has meaning to you and your people! Potential divisions to consider during this decision process include:

◆ Physical structures

◆ Production processes

◆ Product lines

◆ Cost centers

◆ Any combination of the above

Resist the urge to overcomplicate this step. Stay focused on the task: breaking the building up into large blocks. You should have between four and eight logical parts unless you have a very large plant or many variable production processes.

For example, suppose you have a plant similar to the one shown in Figure 3-1 that has three distinct product lines. This mythical plant extrudes plastic strips and then molds (or splices) these strips in a secondary operation. As Figure 3-2 shows, you might break the plant into five parts:

◆ Raw material storage area

◆ Extrusion area

Figure 3-1. Typical plant.

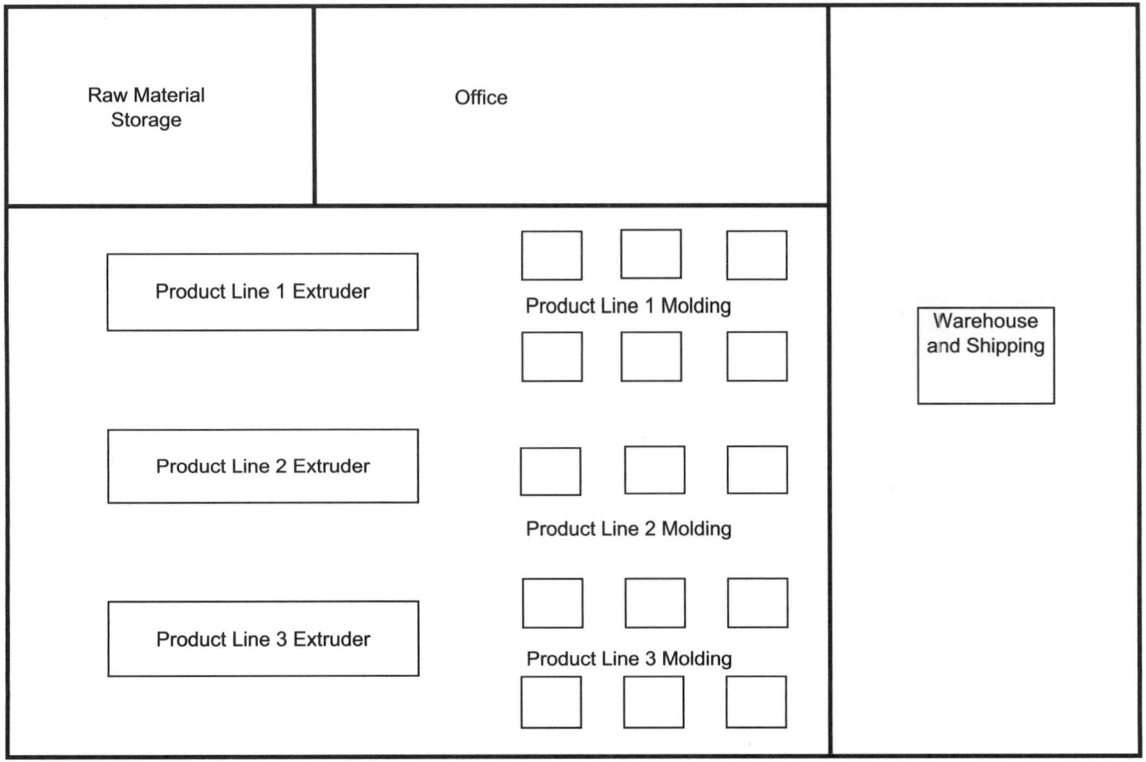

Figure 3-2. Potential plant structure.

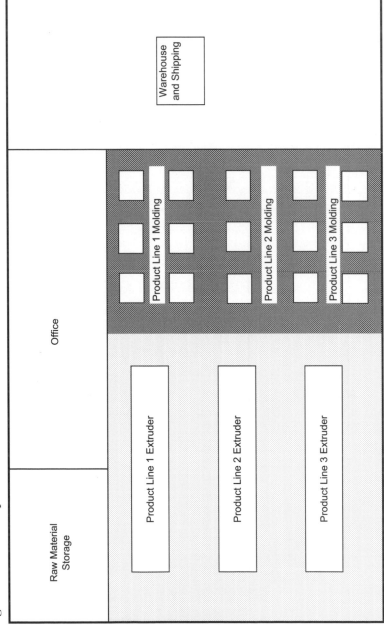

- ◆ Molding area
- ◆ Warehouse
- ◆ Office/common areas

Alternatively, you might break the plant into six parts, as shown in Figure 3-3. In this plant structure, the six areas are:

- ◆ Raw material storage area
- ◆ Product line 1 area
- ◆ Product line 2 area
- ◆ Product line 3 area
- ◆ Warehouse
- ◆ Office/common areas

Physical boundaries, such as walls or separate buildings, will also affect how you define the parts of your building because they affect how you manage your operation and how you stage technicians, repair tools, and parts. Figures 3-4 and 3-5 illustrate how separating walls might be arranged if you were managing your plant operation by process or by product line, respectively. These examples should help you see how the physical structures in your facility will impact your decisions.

HOW DO I START THE PROCESS?

Start the process of defining the plant's logical parts by gathering the implementation team together. Show the group a plant drawing and ask for recommendations on

(text continues on page 45)

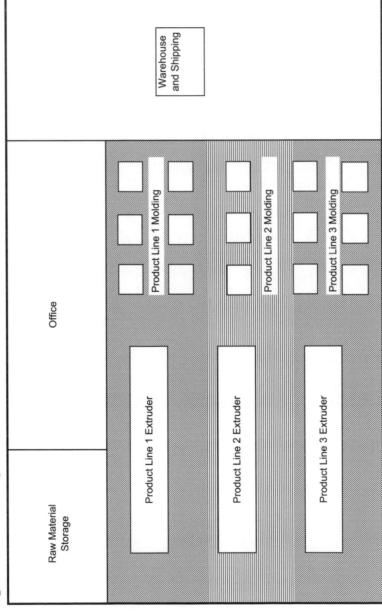

Figure 3-3. Alternative plant structure.

Figure 3-4. Typical plant with walls between process departments.

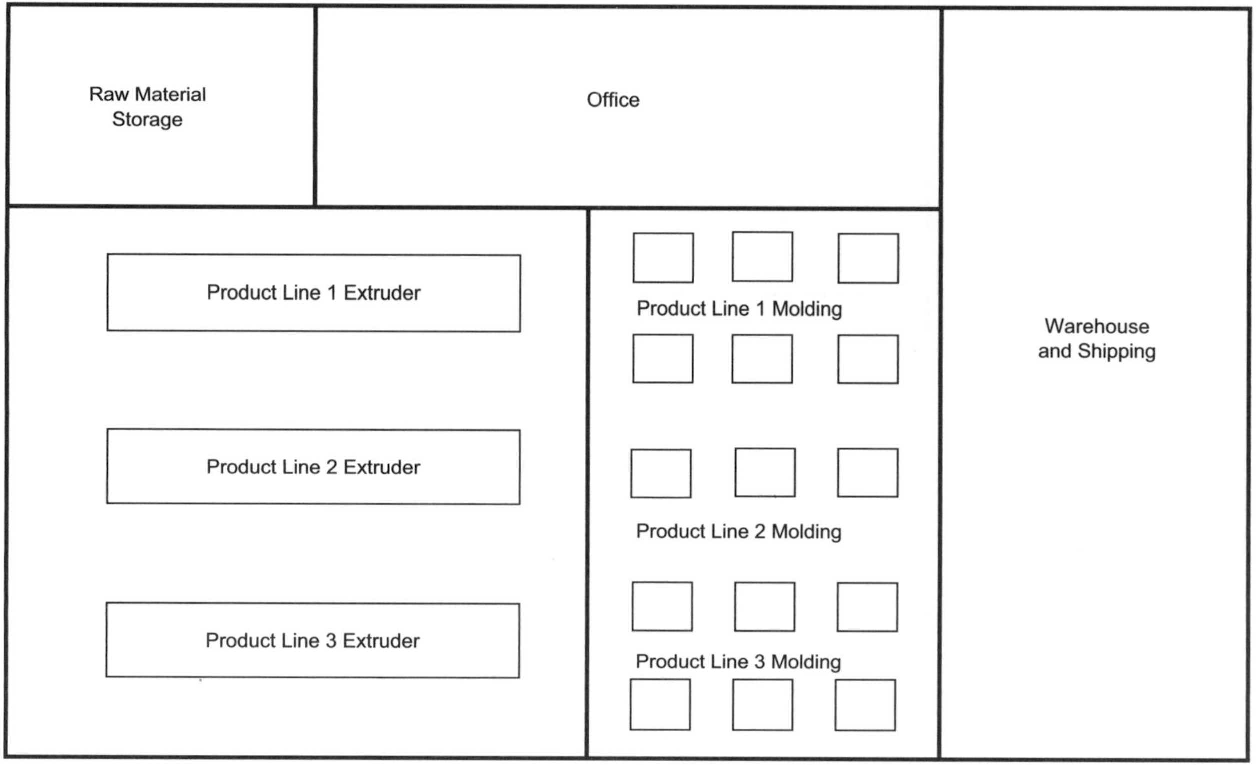

Figure 3-5. Typical plant with walls between product lines.

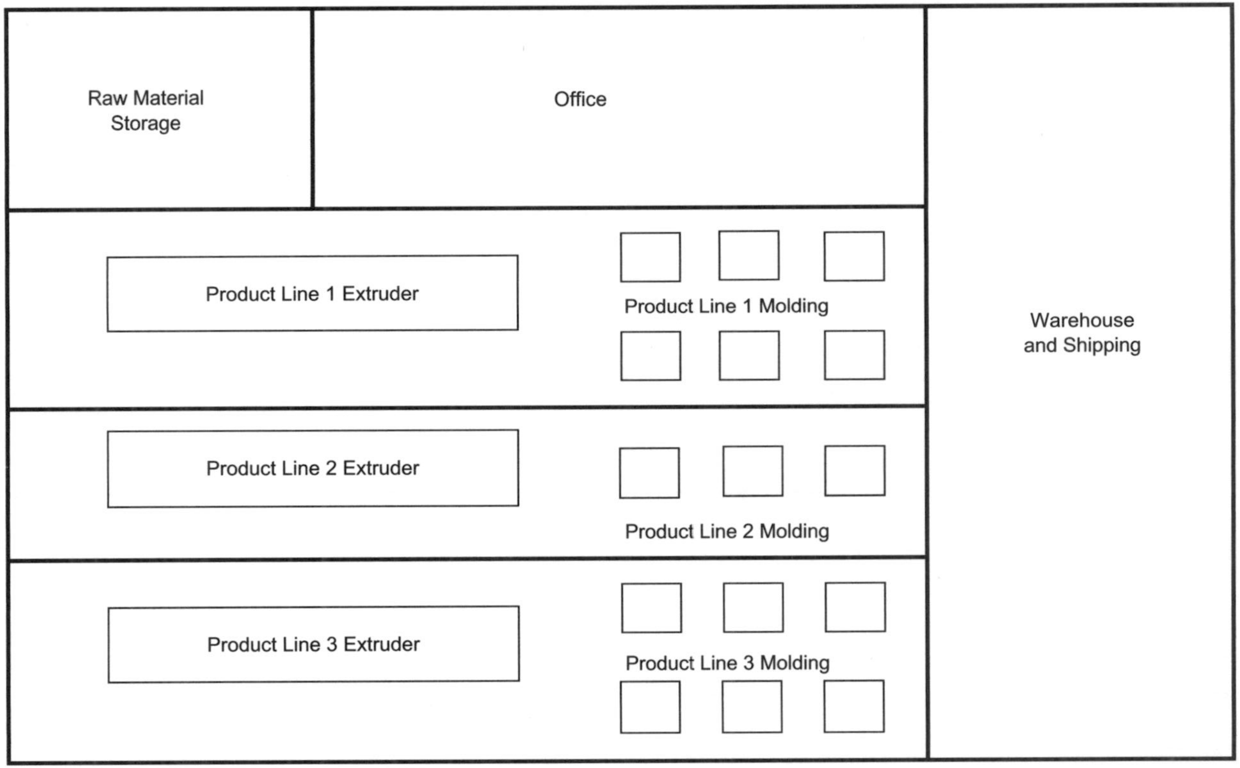

how to break the plant into parts. Discuss some of the "logical" boundaries of the plant. Also discuss some of the implied boundaries within the plant (i.e., those boundaries created by the way you manage the operation). Using this information, identify options and then discuss the pros and cons of each structure. Finally, select the best option that fits your needs.

The "best option" should be easy to explain to all plant personnel and be consistent with how the plant operates. Don't select a structure just because the latest management books say to organize this way!

One word of caution: Expect this step to take longer with a team than if you made the decision by yourself. As with all new teams, the group-formation process must take place. Dismissing this process will prevent the team from maturing and ultimately prevent team members from being able to effectively handle the much tougher jobs of PM workorder development, inventory management, and continuous improvement.

What Do I Do if I Maintain Buildings Instead of Plants?

In this situation, or in circumstances where you have multiple responsibilities, follow the same rationale as people who manage plant maintenance. Look for logical breakpoints based on physical structures, building support systems, and cost centers/processes. For example, you might break a multistory building into exterior grounds, parking garage, plant operations (e.g., HVAC, safety, security), main building, and lobby/elevators.

If the facility has special features, then you should also include them in the list. Special features might be a penthouse restaurant, the shopping mall level, or a hotel. I advise staying away from making each floor a logical part, however. In commercial buildings, also consider what is part of the building and what belongs to the tenants.

If you have responsibility both for separate office buildings and manufacturing/warehouse facilities on the same site, then consider developing parallel structures. If you try to integrate them into one structure, you risk undercutting one or the other operation. (The same logic applies if you are trying to set up a division or corporate-wide structure.) Figure 3-6 shows the recommended relationship.

SUMMARY

A preventive maintenance program begins with breaking up your plant into logical parts. Use the plant's physical structure, production processes, product lines, cost centers, or any combination of these variables as the dividing lines. The selected dividing lines must be meaningful to you and your staff, so tailor the structure to your situation. The selected structure should also reflect how you operate the plant.

Readers with responsibility for office buildings should follow the same advice for developing the logical parts. If you have responsibility for office buildings as well as manufacturing facilities on one site, then consider developing parallel structures.

Do not overcomplicate this step. Instead, use this step

Figure 3-6. Multiple operations require parallel structures.

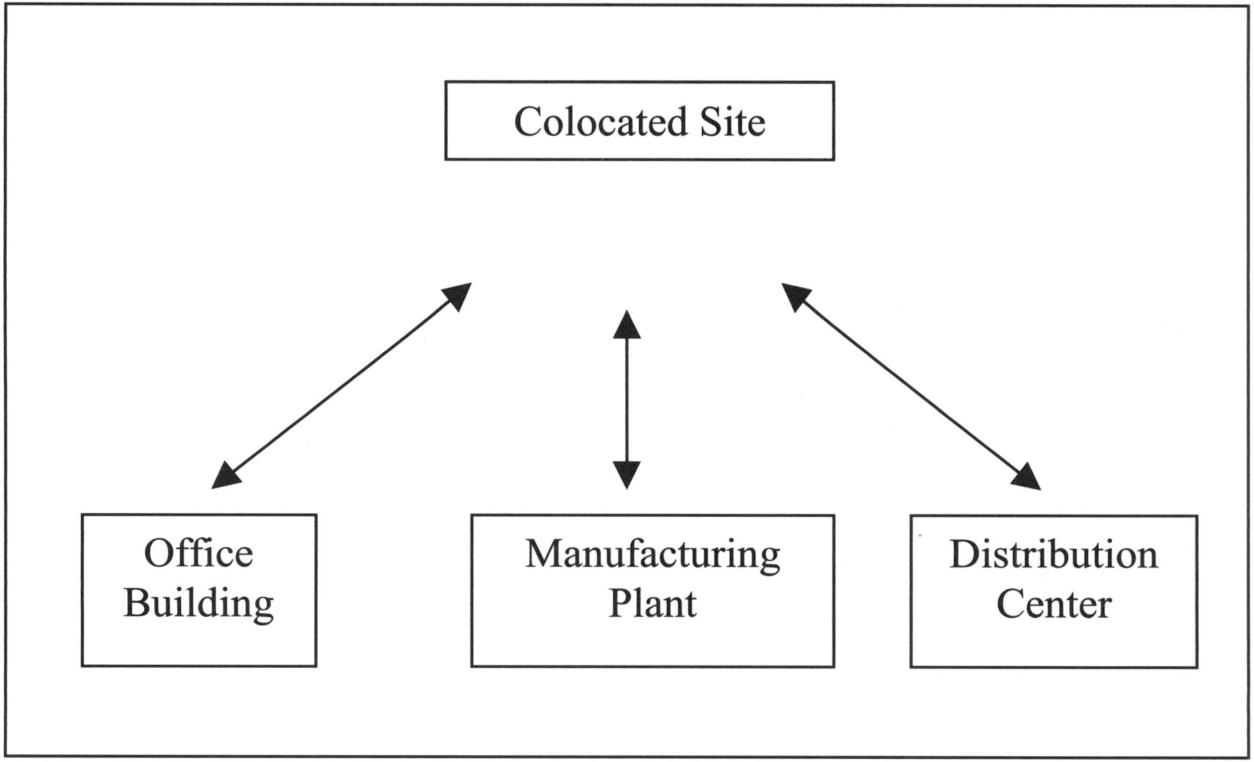

to begin building grassroots support by forming a team to assist in the mapping process.

TEST TIME

This test consists of two questions; see Appendix 5 for answers.

1. Using Figure 3-7 as your reference, propose two options for defining "logical parts" for this plant.

2. How does the addition of a wall in the plant, as shown in the revised plant layout in Figure 3-8, impact your decisions on the structure of the plant?

Figure 3-7. Original plant layout—define the logical parts.

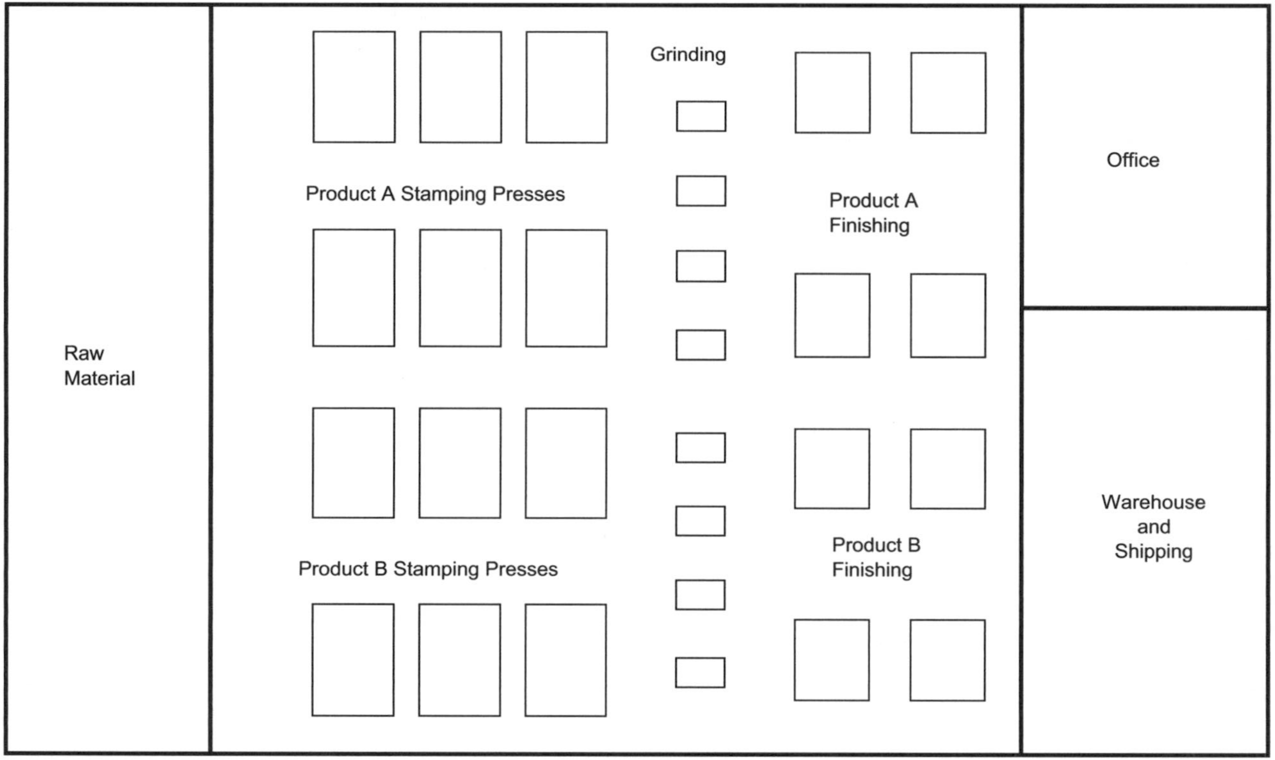

Figure 3-8. *Revised plant layout with walls added.*

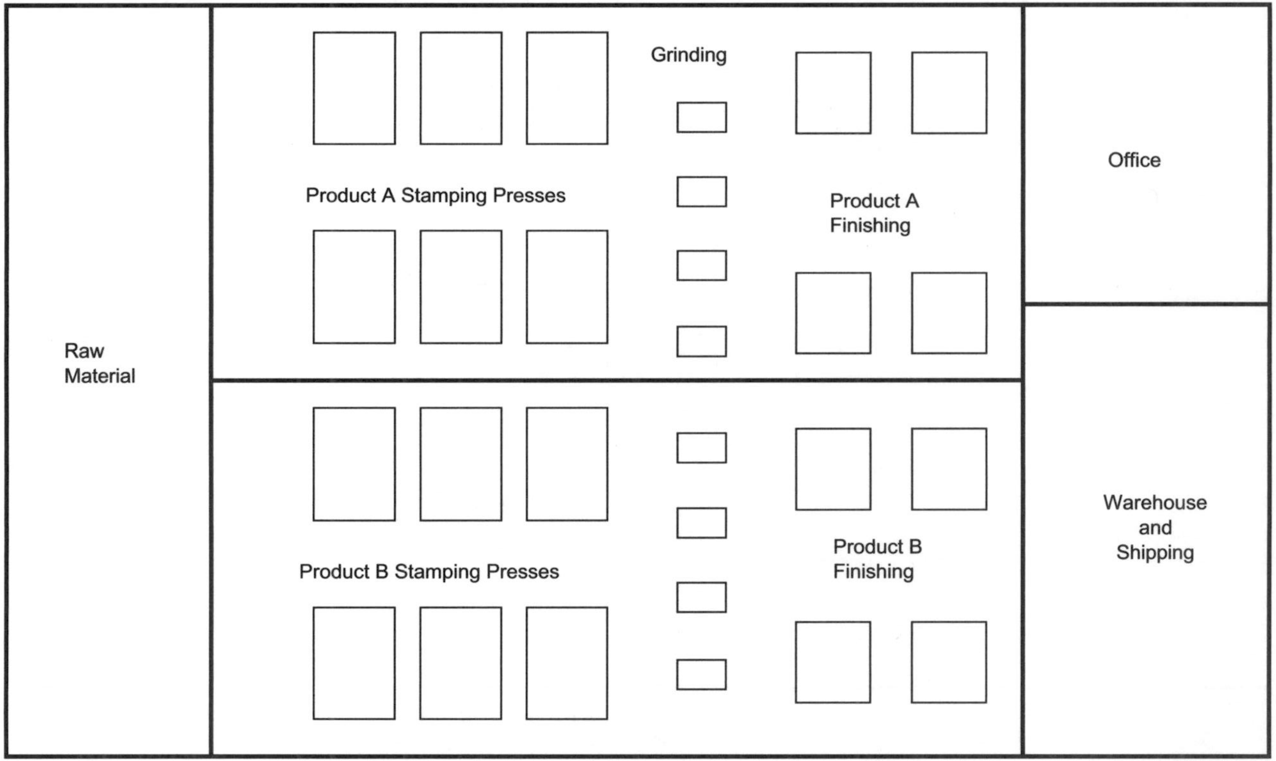

DEVELOPING AN
EQUIPMENT LIST

✓

Are we ever going to get started?

Eventually we will run out to the production floor and write PM work instructions, but first we need to build a numbered equipment list. The "master" equipment list is used to control the flow of workorders and establish a framework to collect equipment history. The master equipment list uses the building structure created in Chapter 3 as its basic framework. Additionally, we will create an equipment numbering structure that represents the plant's uniqueness.

Creation of the master equipment list requires three actions:

1   Developing a numbering system for your plant and the equipment

2   Gathering a list of all the plant's equipment

3   Organizing the equipment into this structure

Once again, don't forget your team when undertaking this process. The input of each team member will ensure a system that everyone understands and supports. To assist in this process, Appendix 2 has a list of generic equipment items you can use to help get the ball rolling.

Developing an equipment list and assigning equipment numbers will also serve as the first test of your new scheduling system. Why is this activity a test? Because this activity probably represents the first time you actually use your workorder and scheduling system beyond the standard repair workorders.

After completing the activities described in Chapter 3 and this chapter, you will have the basic structure for controlling workorders, coupled with the ability to collect trend data by area and by equipment types. (Figure 4-1 shows this relationship pictorially.) The proposed structure recognizes the organizational structure needed for computerized PM programs while still allowing the flexibility to gather data on like equipment pieces common to multiple areas. While these ideas sound intuitive, most PM software companies suggest that you create areas (as in the examples in Chapter 3), then assign equipment specifically to these areas. Later in this chapter, I provide an illustration to clarify the subject. At this junction, if you are not sure where I'm going, then please just read on in blind faith.

Figure 4-1. Breaking the plant into logical parts and numbering equipment by type allows you to "slice and dice" trend data.

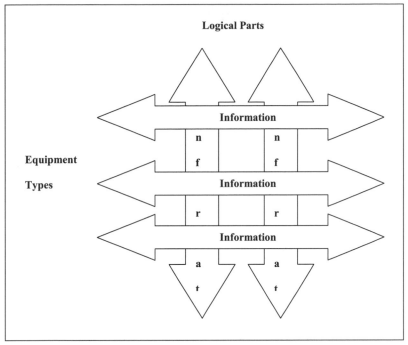

CREATING THE MASTER EQUIPMENT LIST'S STRUCTURE

Before you send everyone out to build equipment lists, you need to develop the list's structure. By developing the structure before you gather the equipment information, you will:

◆ Develop your own expectations of what the final list will look like; this helps to mold the flood of information into a final product.

◆ Be able to communicate to your technicians how the information they collect will be used, which will lead to better first-time list submittals (and reduced editing).

Since the ultimate goal of this chapter is to develop a master equipment list and to assign each piece of equipment a number, we need to discuss the equipment numbers. By equipment numbers, I mean six- or seven-digit numbers (XXX-XXX or XXX-XXXX) that identify equipment type and sequential equipment number. Figure 4-2 clarifies the numbering system.

You don't want to create a unique twelve- or fifteen-digit number with each digit having some meaning. If you did, then only you (and the six clerks you will have to hire) will know what each number means, anyway. Don't try to create another Dewey decimal system, because you will only create a frustrating system that no one understands (or uses).

The first three digits of this numbering scheme can

Figure 4-2. Anatomy of the numbering system.

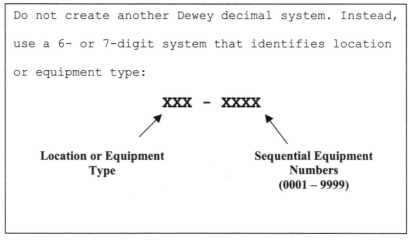

represent locations or equipment types. Whether you select location or equipment type will depend on how you manage your equipment and the amount of commonality between your different pieces of equipment. This decision may also be driven by the desires of the accountants or your manager.

However, the use of locations for the first three digits creates two major problems or limitations:

◆ You cannot readily collect additional trend data on common pieces of equipment that are located in different areas of your plant.

◆ You will need to renumber equipment as you move it within the facility to keep the equipment numbers consistent, which limits the amount of long-term history you can collect. (Additionally, it can cause the accountants heartburn because they think you are pulling a fast one by renumbering equipment.)

I have used both methods and recommend creating a numbering system based on equipment types. Using the equipment type simplifies the process of developing equipment trend data. In addition, depending upon your computerized PM system, entering all of the new PM workorders into the system may be easier.

While trend data may seem like a "nice to have" or a "someday idea," if you continue down the road of professional maintenance management, you will eventually work on improving your system. You may even eventually move into the next phases of preventive maintenance—namely, predictive maintenance, total productive maintenance (TPM), or reliability-centered maintenance (RCM). All of these programs rely on trend data to determine maintenance activities. Furthermore, trend data will identify areas where intervals between overhauls or refurbs can be increased or decreased. Of course, both these actions can save large amounts of money through material and downtime savings or by avoidance of catastrophic failures.

If you choose to use the equipment's location, then plant areas (developed in Chapter 3) or the plant's cost centers should be designated the first three digits. (If your accounting system doesn't readily break out the areas or cost centers with a recognizable three-digit number, then make up your own.) The last three or four digits of the equipment number then come from numbering every piece of equipment in the area or cost center (e.g., 001–999 or 0001–9999).

USING EQUIPMENT TYPE

If you choose to use equipment types, then you need common descriptions with an associated number. The rest of this chapter explains how to set up this system. (Appendix 2 contains a suggested list of equipment numbers to help in this process.)

The equipment type numbering system attempts to name and number common equipment while setting up a structure for naming and numbering process-specific equipment. The proposed structure is:

1XX   Building Equipment
2XX   Generic Process Equipment
3XX–9XX   Process-Specific Equipment

To use these numbers, identify the equipment in the process and establish the three-digit numbers for each *type of equipment*. Next, number each common piece of equipment sequentially. The generic equipment list reserves 300–900 for process-specific items. Use this series of numbers for your additions to the list.

To develop the process-specific equipment numbers, get your group together to select the numbers. Try to remain focused on the big picture. Select the core areas or structures and assign the major digit numbers (e.g., 300, 400, 500, on through 900). Once you have set up the sequence numbers for process-specific equipment, then assign individual three-digit numbers for each piece of unique equipment type (e.g., 310, 311, 312, etc.).

Once again, *do not* complicate this process. Always remember that numbering equipment is a stepping stone to implementing a PM program, not a final destination.

HELPFUL TIP 1

If selecting a sequence becomes an issue, then list all the main categories and assign the numbers by alphabetical order (e.g., 300—Extrusion, 400—Packaging, 500—Raw Material, and so on).

To illustrate these points, let's reexamine the plant we discussed in Chapter 3. Figure 4-3 shows a plant that extrudes plastic, then molds these shapes into the finished products. From Chapter 3, we know that we can divide the building up into several different divisions; however, the processes remain the same. In this example, the equipment numbers required for the office and warehouse/shipping areas are covered by the 1XX and 2XX list in Appendix 2. The raw material storage area may also be

Figure 4-3. Typical plant.

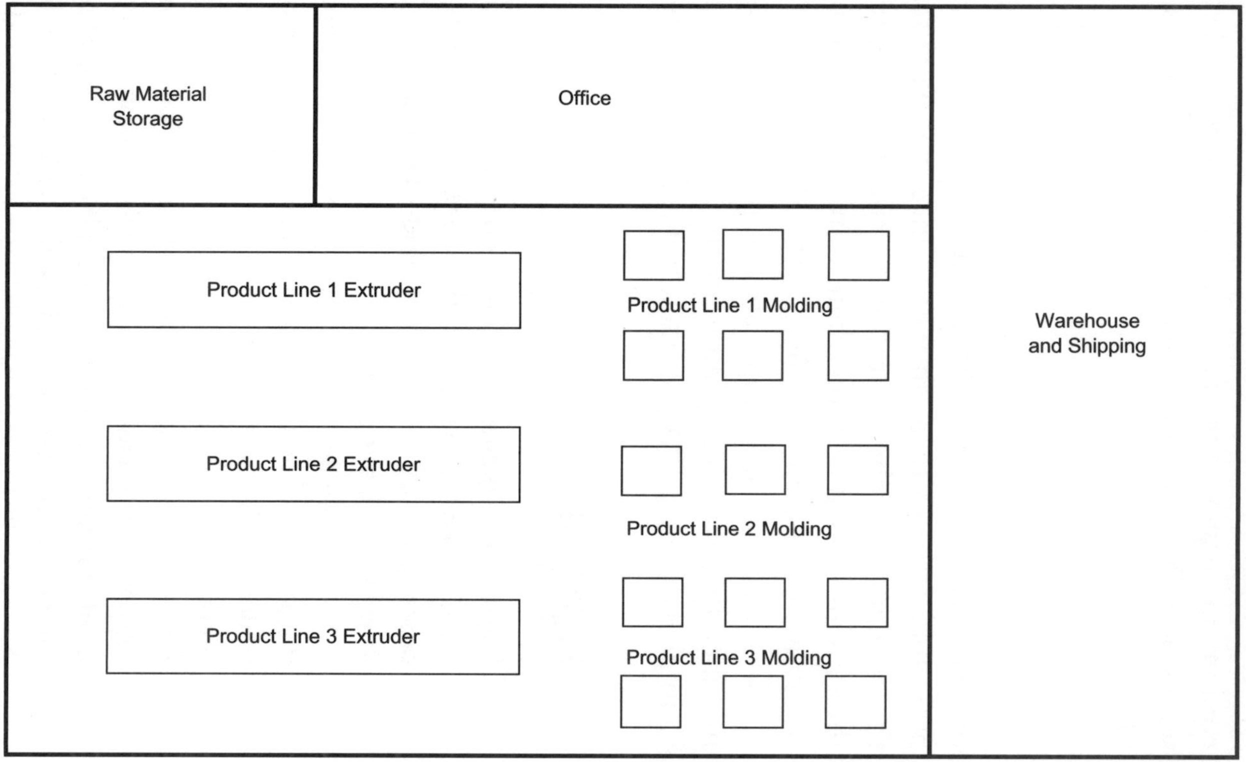

covered by the 1XX and 2XX list in Appendix 2, but may require its own section. The extrusion process and molding process will require their own sections. Therefore, we could assign the equipment numbers as follows:

300 Extrusion Process Equipment

400 Molding Process Equipment

500 Raw Material Storage Equipment

Now that we have our major divisions determined, we are ready to assign specific equipment numbers for each type of process equipment. Continuing with our previous example, let's look at the extrusion process equipment and assign numbers. Suppose the extrusion process consists of an extruder with a feed system, cooling tanks, paint or coating booths, and a saw. This setup might translate into this numbering scheme:

310   Extruder
320   Plastic Feed System
330   Cooling Tank
340   Paint Booth
350   Coating Booth
360   Saw

With this structure in place we can develop a master list of equipment in this area and assign individual equipment numbers. As we make our list we will number all like items sequentially. However, while all extruders will be numbered with the same prefix, they need not have the same name. For our example, the extruders might be named as follows:

310-001   Extruder Line 1, Commercial Products
310-002   Extruder Line 2, Automotive Products
310-003   Extruder Line 3, Construction Products

To determine if an item needs to have its own equipment name and number, use the following guidelines to identify which items should be separated or included in part of a larger system:

◆ Do not break out pumps, motors, or blowers from larger systems unless it adds clarity to describing the system. For example, the 50 HP pumps used for a chilled water loop (shown in Figure 4-4) might be a candidate for breakout while a 100 HP air compressor motor (shown in Figure 4-5) would be included as part of the 100 HP compressor.

◆ For large, complex systems, such as production process lines or conveyors, use physical characteristics to break down the system. For example, an extruder and three-oven curing process might be

Figure 4-4. Give 50 HP pumps their own equipment number and name.

Figure 4-5. Include the 100 HP motor with the compressor.

broken down by equipment into "Extruder, Oven 1, Oven 2, and Oven 3" or, alternatively, into "Extruder and Oven System."

Finally, use a uniform structure for all equipment names. In the previous examples using extruder equipment, we created names using this straightforward structure: "generic equipment, specific name." As another example, consider a plant's #2-200HP air compressor and dryer, which becomes:

221-002   Air Compressor, #2-200 HP
222-002   Air Dryer, #2

(Notice that the three-digit equipment numbers came directly from Appendix 2's generic equipment list.)

When working through the naming process, just remember that you are making this list for your own use, not developing a new naming convention for the world scientific community. Also, use the Helpful Tips offered throughout this chapter to keep the process moving.

HELPFUL TIP 2

Don't fall into the trap of thinking that each process line needs its own three-digit number for each piece of equipment. Develop the three-digit numbers based on the equipment's function rather than make or model.

HELPFUL TIP 3

If you have more than six process areas, then add a digit to the type category. Under these conditions, the equipment number changes from XXX-XXXX to XXXX-XXXX. However, before taking this step, carefully analyze whether you truly have more than six process areas or whether you have failed to properly categorize types.

LET'S NAME EVERYTHING!

After all this upfront organizational work, you are now ready to create a master equipment list. To kick off the process, write workorders that request a list of *all* equipment within each of the newly identified areas. Also, remember to request that workorder assignees follow our simple structure for equipment names: "generic equipment, specific name." And remember to issue each assignee the generic equipment name list in Appendix 2 to assist in the naming process and to avoid duplication.

Now use the scheduling system to get the workorders completed. At this point, you need to be selective about who gets assigned the workorders. Pick people who you believe have the necessary reading and writing skills, the organizational skills, and the knowledge to identify all the equipment in their assigned area. Last but not least, they should possess the maturity, discipline, desire, and motivation to get the workorder completed with a minimum of effort and complaint. In other words, pick winners who will make this part of the effort successful and who will serve as examples for those folks who have not yet broken the code to get the message that planning and scheduling are here to stay.

HELPFUL TIP 4

Using the same technicians to develop the initial list for an entire area will keep the list uniform (rightly or wrongly).

CREATING THE MASTER LIST

When you get the area lists back from the workorder assignees, then compile them into a master list. Once compiled, send this list out for comments and editing. Carefully select the reviewers for their knowledge of the plant and maintenance processes. Also, make sure that everyone on your planning team gets a copy of the draft list. Use this review to pare down the list, combine items, and eliminate extraneous items.

At this point, most people want to schedule a meeting and hash through the whole list. I recommend you wait until you complete at least one review of the list to clean up the spelling errors and duplications. You'll save a lot of time and be spared numerous headaches if you have the reviewers' markup and return of the draft list.

Once you get everyone's comments, then *honestly and open-mindedly,* review their recommendations and decide whether to accept or reject their comments. Be prepared to justify (or defend) why you chose not to accept a reviewer's comments. Also, as part of this first review, get rid of or combine trivial items that some people feel compelled to include, such as the "red boiler chemical fill bucket." (Do not smirk until you have seen your list for the first time.) Only after you have reviewed and combined everybody's comments are you ready to schedule a meeting to prepare a final master equipment list.

HELPFUL TIP 5

The process of developing an equipment list is another opportunity to bring people on board with the program or kick them off the train. When you create the equipment list, try not to be too critical. Make sure you have a complete list, but give the people making the list some leeway.

HELPFUL TIP 6

Do not be too quick to delete those safety items that require periodic inspections—for example, ladders, safety harnesses, and pressure relief valves. Having these items numbered not only helps to ensure these inspections get done through the issuance of PM workorders, but also allows you to generate a workorder history for the safety and insurance inspectors. Use your judgment.

HELPFUL TIP 7

Let the production folks take a look at the list. Not only does this help to get them on board, but it also allows you to verify that maintenance and production share the same view of the building. (They may even have a few good ideas!)

HELPFUL TIP 8

The first time you number the plant's equipment, number all the like equipment pieces sequentially as they "sit" in the plant. As an example, try to avoid numbering "Air Handler, Boiler 1" as 110-001 and "Air Handler, Boiler 2" as 110-012. Sequential numbering makes it easier for the technicians when they start using the PM workorders. After the first pass, you will not be able to follow this sequential process, but by then you will have seasoned people. The difference in numbers will also serve to identify the newer pieces of equipment.

PUTTING EQUIPMENT NUMBERS ON EQUIPMENT

Finally, once all the equipment has been assigned numbers, then issue workorders to label each piece of equipment with its newly assigned number. Labeling equipment can be as simple as painting the numbers on the equipment or as complicated as creating special labels. For instance, a maintenance superintendent who includes a barcode on his tags (see Figure 4-6) anticipates using handheld computers in the future. Figure 4-7 shows another type of special label that includes not only the equipment

Figure 4-6. Example of an equipment tag with a barcode.

Figure 4-7. Sample equipment tag.

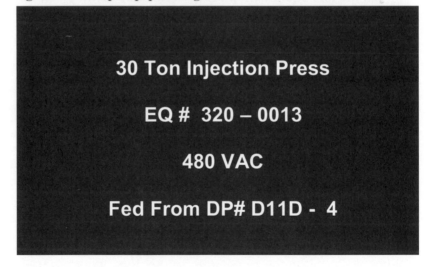

name and number, but also the incoming voltage and electrical feed panel location.

The guidance in the Helpful Tips should make the process of labeling your equipment go easier—and you may avoid some of the mistakes I've made along the way.

HELPFUL TIP 9

Initially use plastic tape to get the numbers on the equipment—even if you plan to have special tags made for your

equipment. (Avoid duct tape since it will leave tape residue on the machine when you remove it.) There will be an inevitable delay with the first order of tags. It usually takes time to get the style and format correct. It also takes time for a vendor to produce a large quantity of special tags. Do not add confusion to the PM program implementation by waiting for everything to be perfect before putting numbers on the equipment.

If you decide to have special tags made, make sure you are happy with the final design before placing the final order or giving production go ahead. Don't be afraid to see a production-quality draft of the tags. (Given the price of these little puppies, you do not want to receive 200 to 300 tags with the wrong format or wrong logo.)

HELPFUL TIP 10

Avoid using paper or vinyl labels. They do not hold up in the typical plant environment and the writing eventually fades. (Trust me, I've made this mistake.)

HELPFUL TIP 11

Before ordering tags, discuss your plans with the plant controller, who may want the company's capital equipment number included on each tag. This number is typically eight to twenty digits long and usually has no relationship to any numbering system on this planet. The purpose for including this number on the tag is that it will simplify the company's required periodic capital equipment audits.

Do not, however, allow the plant's controllers to talk you into using their number in place of your number. Typically, the accountants have no idea of what you are trying to accomplish or the challenges of implementing professional maintenance management.

SUMMARY

Before you start writing PM work instructions, develop a master equipment list that includes all the equipment in your plant or plants. After completing the activities in Chapter 3 and this chapter, you will then have the basic structure for controlling workorders, coupled with the ability to collect trend data by area and by equipment types. The proposed structure recognizes the organizational structure needed for computerized PM programs while still allowing the flexibility to gather data on like equipment pieces located in multiple areas.

The key points to remember are:

◆ Create the structure of the master equipment list before sending your technicians out to gather the equipment information.

◆ Keep the numbering system simple by limiting the numbers to six or seven digits (XXX-XXX or XXX-XXXX).

◆ Try to use generic names and try to be as complete as possible.

◆ Assign the equipment numbers by equipment type, if possible, rather than equipment location. If you choose to assign numbers by equipment type, then Appendix 2 contains a numbering convention option you may find most useful. If you choose to assign numbers by equipment location, then try to use an existing three- or four-digit numbering system that has some meaning to the existing plant operation; for example, you might use cost center numbers.

◆ Use the workorder scheduling system to get the equipment list information. Be selective about who gets these workorders to ensure quality of the data submitted.

◆ Put your newly assigned equipment numbers on each piece of equipment. If you want to create special tags, then use some interim method (i.e., tape) to put the numbers on the equipment while finalizing the special tags.

◆ Don't get hung up on the process when creating your numbering system. Keep the numbering simple. Avoid the urge to create a numbering system that uses special definitions that require a Ranger Rick decoder ring to understand.

◆ Remember that this activity represents another opportunity to build consensus and create buy-in within your maintenance group.

TEST TIME

This test consists of three questions; see Appendix 5 for answers.

1. How would you assign equipment number prefixes for the plant shown in Figure 4-8?

2. Should the pumps in the chiller system in Figure 4-9 be part of the larger system's numbering scheme or should you give them their own equipment number?

3. Would you give the ladder in Figure 4-10 its own equipment number?

Figure 4-8. Assign equipment numbers for this plant.

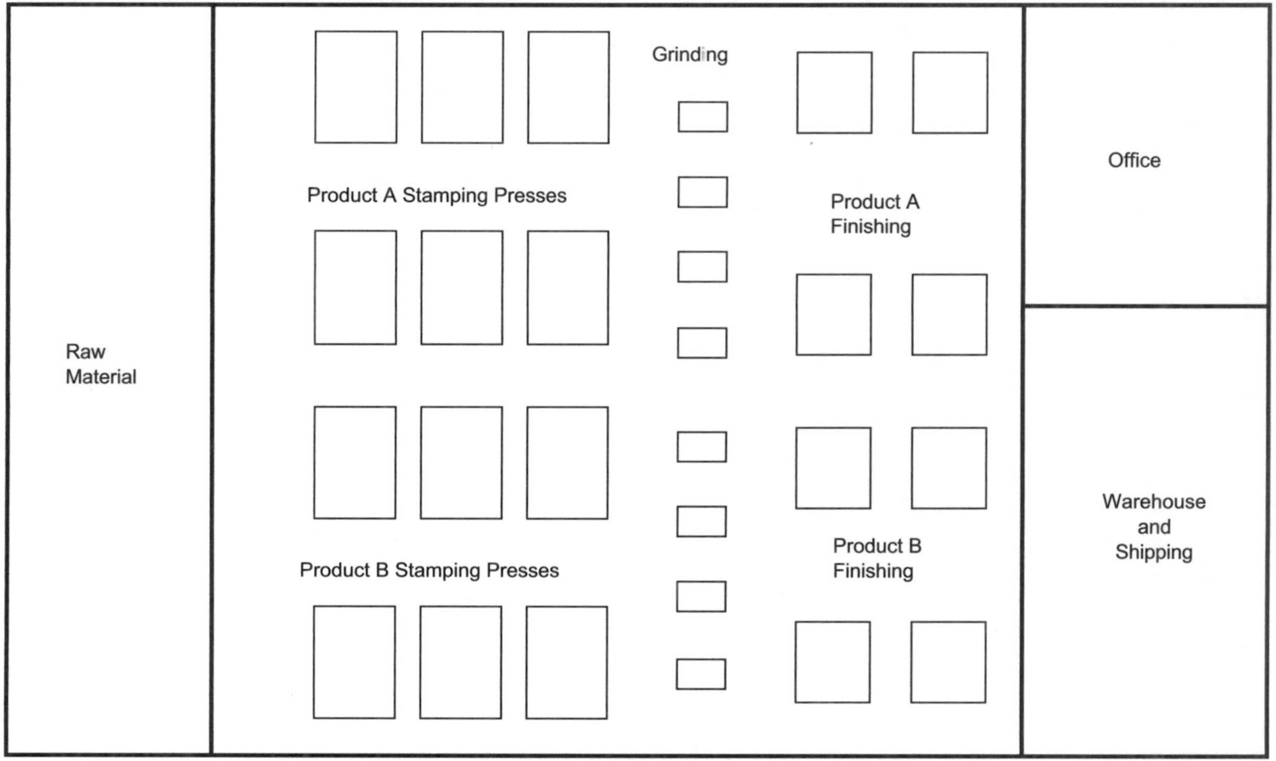

Figure 4-9. Should the pumps have their own equipment number?

Figure 4-10. To number or not to number?

WRITING PMs

Let the party begin . . .

Kids, we're here! We are now ready to write preventive maintenance (PM) workorders! In my opinion, after committing to the scheduling process, writing the PM workorders is the hardest part of developing a PM program. Some of the pitfalls or challenges include the fear of writing (or, at the other extreme, the desire to write a workorder version of *War and Peace*), an unwillingness to share information, and fears about the immensity of the task. Fortunately, all these problems are solvable, and the reward of having a PM system far outweighs any challenges associated with startup.

EAT THE ELEPHANT ONE BITE AT A TIME

If you want to succeed in this phase, my advice is to keep it simple. Start the process by looking at your newly developed equipment list and creating groupings of identical equipment. Once you identify the largest groups of identical equipment, write workorders to get PMs developed for these groups.

In a typical factory, the first twenty workorders will cover 50 percent to 75 percent of the factory. Using the scheduling process developed in Chapter 2, you can schedule the workorders for completion. As you complete one equipment group, move to the next group.

To ensure your PM authors deliver a complete product, use the form in Appendix 3, which is structured to support the process outlined in the rest of this chapter. The form uses multiple pages (one page for each interval) to make review and typing easier.

HELPFUL TIP 1

If you have limited resources or you truly have no identical equipment, then pick the piece of equipment or the process line with the greatest amount of downtime. When you finish writing PMs for this piece of equipment or process line, then start on the next piece of equipment or process line with the greatest amount of downtime, and so on and so on.

When you schedule workorders for creation of PM instructions, you also need to carefully select the person to write the PMs for each piece of equipment. Try to pick "experts" who:

◆ Can read and write well

◆ Will ask others for their opinions and help

◆ Are not afraid to share their own personal knowledge

Stress to your PM authors the importance of using all available resources for writing their assigned PM. These resources include their own expertise, other technicians' and operators' expertise, the equipment manuals, general technical information, and the equipment vendor. Do not underestimate the need for the writers to research and coordinate good PMs. If you have the choice between a prima donna expert and a "lesser" expert who can communicate, then pick the lesser expert. Remember, one of your goals in developing the PM system should be to convert everyone's personal/private knowledge into public knowledge. You will only reduce downtime and eliminate firefighting by taking the magic out of the PM process.

HELPFUL TIP 2

If you decide to choose people who have considerable expertise but who cannot write, or do so poorly, then help them author the PMs by doing the writing for them. If you opt for ghostwriting, it should be done with courtesy, respect, and confidentiality.

HELPFUL TIP 3

Consider tapping your insurance company for advice on building PM workorders. All the questions that insurers ask on their annual inspections don't come out of thin air, so turn your insurance company into a resource. Insurance companies usually have guidelines for checking sprinkler systems, ventilation systems, boilers, and general safety equipment.

ELEMENTS OF A PM PROCEDURE

What makes up a good PM workorder? That's easy—just write everything down! Wrong! Good PM workorder instructions contain all of the following components:

◆ All the required safety steps
◆ All the "definitive sequential steps"
◆ All the required equipment readings and settings
◆ All the required tools
◆ All the required replacement parts (by part number, size, or some other applicable description)

Create a separate workorder for each PM interval (e.g., weekly, monthly, semiannually, etc.). Also, make running and nonrunning PMs into separate workorders for each interval.

The PM Procedure Worksheet in Appendix 3 is designed to help you get the necessary information in the proper interval. As formatted, these sheets are the basis for the creation of the individual interval operating and nonoperating workorders. Don't be intimidated by the multipage format of Appendix 3. By developing the information in this format, the PM workorder authors will be able to create the individual interval (e.g., weekly, monthly, quarterly) workorders during their original submittal.

WRITING GOOD INSTRUCTIONS

What are "definitive sequential steps"? They are all the steps necessary to perform a specific maintenance activity from start to finish. Each step is a specific action required to complete the desired task. Each step should:

◆ Start with an action word (e.g., lockout, measure, pour, remove, reinstall, etc.).

◆ Include specific details to avoid confusion or mistakes.

◆ Be simple and objective (i.e., avoid the urge to write a ten-line definitive sequential step).

◆ List any parts needed for the step.

If appropriate, reference or attach a drawing to provide clarity. Figure 5-1 is an example of workorder instructions for checking chainstretch.

HELPFUL TIP 4

Put blank lines in front of each step on the workorder so the technician can check off each step as completed. The checkmarks will:

Figure 5-1. An example of definitive sequential steps.

____ Lockout machine power at panel DP3, breaker 5.

____ Remove and stretch out drive chain on floor.

____ Measure length of 20 chain links, and record reading.
    Twenty chain links = _____.

____ Replace chain, if length is greater than 17.5 inches with Part #800906.

____ Retime machine using vendor drawing #875498, Rev 4 to show the proper timing mark locations.

____ Remove lockout from machine.

____ Confirm machine timing.

◆ Indicate whether the technician followed the steps as listed

◆ Serve as a memory jogger if the technician gets called away before completing the workorder

TURNING THE DRAFT INTO FINAL PM WORKORDERS

As technicians complete workorders, then someone will need to edit the instructions and create the individual PM work instructions. (Note I said "someone," not specifically you.) The editor should read each sheet for clarity and logical flow. The editor should also look for the following items:

◆ Are proper safety instructions listed?

◆ Are the instructions clear on running vs. nonrunning activities?

◆ Are the instructions listed in the proper interval?

◆ Are the steps listed in a logical and understandable sequence?

◆ Are the details provided sufficient for each step? (For example, an instruction to "Lubricate five points" is more useful than saying "Grease press.")

If the workorder is missing information, then return it to the author so the necessary information can be added. If the workorder simply needs its grammar polished, then make the changes and move on.

HELPFUL TIP 5

Avoid getting bogged down when trying to get all the settings, measurements, and part numbers for the workorders. Leave a blank on the workorder for the missing data (e.g., "Replace with _____ photoeye") and have the technicians fill in the blanks when they perform the work for the first time.

HELPFUL TIP 6

As time passes, you may want to change information on the workorders or add missing detail. Use Helpful Tip 5 to gather the necessary values and readings by writing a note with your request for more information.

HELPFUL TIP 7

Since writing all the PM workorders will take some time, consider making a master list of all the PM workorders. Use this list as a management tool to make sure you get the workorders done and that you don't forget any pieces of equipment. Consider using the format in Figure 5-2 to track your progress in writing PM workorders.

Figure 5-2. Master list format for PM workorders.

Equipment Group	Workorder #	Date Scheduled	% Complete	Date Completed

When creating the draft work instructions, be careful to avoid mixing intervals within one PM workorder. For example, don't write "change oil every third month" on a monthly PM workorder because it is a quarterly PM workorder instruction. Let your PM system manage the intervals for you. Do not get caught in the trap of thinking "we did this last time," with the last time being a year ago, instead of three months!

PM Workorders Are Not Limited to Maintenance Departments

Don't be afraid to let other departments have workorders included in the system. Recognize that a good PM system is faceless—it does not care who gets PMs. The intent of the PM system is to get the work done and to have a history of the work. Other departments that may want to be included in the PM system include production, safety, and sanitation.

If you want to include other departments in the PM system, then meet with the managers of these departments to discuss your proposal. Ask them for input and participation. Agree on who will provide draft PMs. Also agree on how the PMs will be issued and managed. Finally, reassure them that this offer is not your attempt to take over the plant.

Scheduling PMs

Once you have the PM work instructions completed, then you need to establish the start date of each PM workorder. Gee, that's pretty obvious—or is it? While it may appear obvious, many people do not recognize the need to stagger the start dates of the workorders to avoid creating a monthly tidal wave.

When creating the PM schedule, consider how the PMs will fit into the plant's production schedule. For example, if you have ten machines, each with a weekly, monthly, and semiannual PM workorder, your options are to:

1 Spread the PMs evenly over specified intervals to avoid shutting down the entire plant at any given time. Scenarios might be to schedule:

◆ Two machines each day for their weekly PM

◆ Two or three machines each week for their monthly PM

◆ One or two machines each month for their semiannual PM

2 Schedule all ten machines on the same week for their monthly and semiannual PMs, provided you have regularly scheduled plant downtime.

Finally, don't worry about which machines get preventive maintenance inspections first in the initial sequence. If you faithfully do the PMs as scheduled, then staggering the PMs between the various machines usually doesn't matter. If you have the resources, then you should perform the semiannual PMs and the annual PMs at the start of the program.

Quality Assurance of PM Write-Ups

Once you have written PM instructions and have set up the initial start dates, then you are finally ready to start executing the PM program. Use this start-up period as a honeymoon—and be prepared for the following responses from your technicians:

◆ Not understanding the work instruction

◆ Disagreement with the steps or the order

◆ Disagreement with the inspection parameters

Expect these issues to pop up. In this light, you might even ask the assigned technicians to critique the work-order for suggested changes and corrections when you schedule the workorders for the first time. Also make sure they understand the intent of the assigned work-order. Finally, be sensitive to their comments about the workorders.

As you receive feedback, evaluate it for potential changes to the workorders or the system. Accept the feedback for what it is—a way to improve the quality of the workorders—and don't take it as an attack on you as a person, as a supreme maintenance being, or as an intellect. By actively seeking feedback (and keeping it in perspective), you will not only improve the workorders, you'll also create another opportunity to generate buy-in.

Here is the flip side of this recommendation: In every organization, there are some poor souls who have never had a happy day in their entire lives. Don't let them use any imperfections in the system as an opportunity to sabotage the program by arguing over semantics and names or knitpicking over "happy" for "glad" wording choices.

◆ *Politically correct advice:* Be ready to manage or channel their feedback.

◆ *Politically incorrect translation:* Everyone needs to know you welcome suggestions to improve the program. However, if all they want to do is complain, then they should shut up and get back to work.

SUMMARY

Once you have created the required program structure, then you are ready to write PM work instructions. Use the scheduling system to get the PM workorders written. Be selective about who you assign to write the workorder instructions—pick people who know the piece of equipment, want to help launch the program, and last but not least, can communicate.

Keep the workorder format simple. A good PM workorder lists:

- ◆ All the required safety steps
- ◆ All the definitive sequential steps
- ◆ All the required readings and settings
- ◆ All the required tools
- ◆ All the required replacement parts (by part number, size, or some other applicable description)

Put the steps in checklist format and use action words to start each step. Put blank lines in front of each step so the technician can check off each step as completed. Create a separate workorder for each PM interval (i.e., weekly, monthly, semiannually) and for running and nonrunning PMs. Do not allow different PM intervals to sneak onto the same workorder (i.e., don't put quarterly instructions on the monthly PM). Issue each PM author the PM Procedure Worksheet in Appendix 3 to ensure you get all this information into the desired format.

Once you have the workorders created, then schedule their first occurrence. When scheduling the first occurrence, spread out the workorders over the appropriate interval to develop a level workload. Once you have set up the first occurrence, then let the system "kick them out" at the proper interval.

Finally, as the actual program begins, use this time to improve and correct the workorders. Actively seek feedback on how to improve the workorders and the system.

TEST TIME

Your test is to critique some written PM instructions; see Appendix 5 for answers.

1. Here are three instructions that are included on a monthly PM workorder. Identify what is wrong with each of these "definitive steps":
   a. Lubricate press using synthetic high-temp grease.
   b. Change air filter every sixth month.
   c. Change oil using four gallons of Smithcon 360 oil.

2. Describe how to improve the following workorder:

Air Filter Inspection and Filter Change

_____ Check air house magnahelic gauge and change filters if reading is too high.
_____ Verify fan motor off.
_____ Replace filters.
_____ Turn fan motor back on.

6

DEVELOPING EQUIPMENT MANUALS

✓

*Manuals? We don't need any
stinking manuals!*

If you ask a group of maintenance managers, "Do you
have manuals for your equipment?" all will respond,
"Yes, of course." And yes, in truth, they have manuals,
but only about 10 percent have "real" manuals. I define
a real manual as one containing:

- ◆ Operating procedures
- ◆ Troubleshooting guide
- ◆ Schematics
- ◆ PLC program (if applicable)
- ◆ Parts lists
- ◆ Other significant items (e.g., manuals for specific
  process control equipment)

WHY DO WE NEED MANUALS?

"Why do we need these manuals? We have been using our books for years," many will say.

Manuals round out your maintenance management program. They give you the troubleshooting information necessary to solve those complex problems that cannot be solved by the usual "little tweak" or "switch flipping." With real manuals in your shop, when an uncommon or complex problem arises, then you will have the necessary information on hand to quickly troubleshoot it.

HELPFUL TIP 1

To cut down on your troubleshooting time:

◆ Place equipment documentation in your control panels.

◆ Laminate copies of the electrical schematics and post them on the inside of the machine's electrical door panel (as shown in Figure 6-1).

◆ Copy drawings of the PLC I/O modules and color in the I/O lights that should be lit for various operations. Laminate these newly created pictures and post them next to the electrical schematics in the control panel.

HELPFUL TIP 2

To help in the machine lockout process and to improve compliance, post the lockout instructions for each machine on the door of each machine's control panel. This action not only simplifies the lockout process, but also raises safety awareness. (Figure 6-2 shows a 100-ton C-Frame

Figure 6-1. Electrical schematic and PLC diagram posted inside the electrical panel door (colored to show which module lights are on during a normal startup).

press with its lockout procedures posted on the control panel.)

When you implement this tip, be sure to add an instruction to all monthly equipment PM workorders to verify that lockout instructions are posted on each machine.

How Do We Create These Manuals?

Manuals are created the same way you get everything else done—you write workorders and schedule them! To set up the workorders, go back to the master list of all PM workorders (which you developed in Chapter 5).

Figure 6-2. Electrical panel with the machine's lockout instructions posted on the outside of the door.

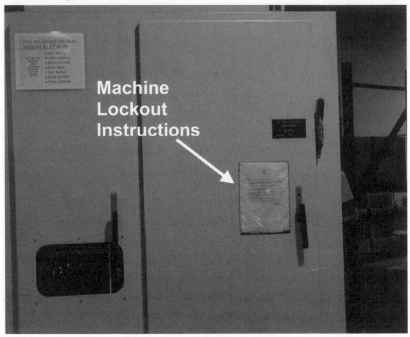

Target manual development for common pieces of equipment and also large items such as process lines or building systems.

Once you have the list, get your staff to create the manuals. As with every other part of this implementation program, you want to have your staff involved in making recommendations on the best way to break down the items.

Also, as in the PM writing process, carefully pick who gets assigned these workorders. Make sure the person has the necessary aptitude and skills to create a good manual. These workorders are just as important as performing PM workorders on a multimillion-dollar piece of equipment.

Remember, after all, *you plan to use these manuals to repair that multimillion-dollar piece of equipment.*

HELPFUL TIP 3

Create a master list of all the workorders related to the creation of your manuals. Use this list to track status and to make sure the work gets done.

Use a format similar to the one proposed in Chapter 5 (Figure 5-2) that you used to track your progress in writing PM workorders.

WHERE DO WE GET THE MATERIAL FOR THESE MANUALS?

The material for the manual comes from the existing manuals and drawings. Start with the manuals you already have in the shop. In most cases, you will have several copies of the same manuals, all at different levels of completeness. I recommend you take these manuals, break them apart, and make copies of the parts you need. Once you have copies of what you need, then place them in a binder with the appropriate dividers. If you do not have everything you need, then call the original equipment vendor and request the material you're missing.

HELPFUL TIP 4

Put all the manuals in the same color binders and store them by equipment number in a central library. The

matching binders give the manuals a professional appearance that goes along with your new approach to maintenance.

The use of standardized colors also makes inventorying the manuals and spotting them on the floor easier.

HELPFUL TIP 5

While you're creating the manuals, it is also the perfect time to verify that you have commented backup copies of all computer programs.

HELPFUL TIP 6

Consider using employees on restricted duty to develop the manuals. Using people on light duty helps out the human resources department while providing you with some "free" labor. If you follow this tip, be selective about whom you accept for the project. Also, have some example manuals on hand for them to use as a guide.

WHAT GOES IN THE MANUAL UNDER THE "OTHER SIGNIFICANT ITEMS" HEADING?

Put any unique information in this section. Examples include manuals for process control items such as temperature controllers and timers, or special information on PLC hardware (e.g., thermocouple modules, molding modules) or drives. Usually the above-mentioned items come with a manual of their own. You can get this information by going to one of several sources:

- The original manual
- The department pack rats who think they need one of everything
- The local equipment distributor

One other alternative exists for getting this information. If you have spares for any of these items, then get the manual from their packing box. Use this manual to make copies, then return the manual to the packing box.

WHAT ARE TROUBLESHOOTING GUIDES?

In my experience, the toughest part of developing equipment manuals is creating the troubleshooting guide. If you become serious about your manuals, or if you have highly specialized equipment, then you should create your own troubleshooting guide. In that case, consider using this four-part format:

1 Potential problems or symptoms

2 Potential causes

3 Corrective action for each cause

4 Required parts

Figure 6-3 is an example of how to use this troubleshooting guide format. List the potential causes of problems and corrective actions from "most likely and easiest to fix" to "least likely and most difficult to fix." Also, heed the advice from Chapter 5 on writing PM work-orders to make sure you end up with a usable product. For instance:

Figure 6-3. Sample troubleshooting guide.

Troubleshooting Guide for 300 Ton ABC Presses

Potential Problem or Symptom	Potential Causes	Corrective Actions	Parts
Machine will not cycle.	Control power not turned on.	Press green start button.	
	Safety light curtain activated.	Check light curtain indicator light (located to the left of the Panel Mate screen). If red light is on, then check for obstructions and remove.	
	Panel breaker tripped.	Check breaker and reset. Monitor to determine cause of original trip.	
	Mold position limit switch not made.	Mold not properly positioned. Check position and correct if required.	
		Limit switch not operating properly. Check for proper positioning and operation.	PN# J67459; plant stores number: 234-5894

Continue the process of identifying symptoms and causes.

List sequence of actions:
- Be specific
- Do not forget safety

List all required parts to make corrective action.

◆ Use action words (e.g., check, measure, adjust, etc.).

◆ Include specific details to avoid confusion or mistakes.

◆ Keep it simple and objective (i.e., avoid the urge to write a ten-line troubleshooting step).

◆ List any parts needed for each item.

HELPFUL TIP 7

On future equipment purchases, request a troubleshooting guide and recommended PM instructions as part of the purchase. By requesting the guide and the PM list, you reduce the amount of work required to create the new manuals. This information will also help speed up getting the new equipment into production.

Be advised that this special purchase request may not apply to off-the-shelf hardware. However, with the increased focus on ISO standards, many equipment manufacturers have improved their manuals by adding PM recommendations and troubleshooting information.

HELPFUL TIP 8

Use the new troubleshooting guide to review existing PM workorders and make changes as appropriate.

Developing the troubleshooting guide gives you new insights into potential failures, which allows you to create better PMs and to identify required spare parts.

HELPFUL TIP 9

Set up a special work area for manual creation. This area doesn't need to be an office or conference room; it just needs to be a space where the different manual pieces can be spread out and worked on. This area also reserves a space where the work-in-progress manuals may be left out between workdays.

In addition, it becomes a lot easier for supervisors and team leaders to keep track of their "manual creators" if they are given a special work area.

Reviewing, Editing, and Maintaining the Manuals

Editing and quality control are the last steps in the manual-creation process. The manual must be reviewed for completeness and neatness. During this review, make sure the information is accurate and up to date.

Once you have all the information for the manual gathered together and you have ensured the manual is in fact complete, then guard it with your life. Put the originals in a master library. For easy identification, follow Helpful Tip 4 and select a unique color for the master manuals. Use the master manuals to make replacement copies for the shop manuals. Also, make it perfectly clear to one and all, that *no one* takes a master copy out of the library except to copy or in an emergency.

It is equally important to keep the contents of the manuals updated. An easy way to keep them current is by issuing a semiannual inspection PM for each shop manual. This inspection workorder should be used to verify the completeness of all pages/sections, as well as their condition. If something is missing or in bad shape (e.g., torn, stained, or damaged such that the information can't be read), then go to the master copy and make replacement copies. If you get new information that should go in the manuals, then write a workorder for it to be added into both the master copy and the shop copy.

Summary

The creation of manuals is the final step in the setup of the maintenance management process. Good documentation that's well organized in equipment manuals makes the job of troubleshooting faster and easier. A good manual contains:

◆ Operating procedures
◆ Troubleshooting guide
◆ Schematics
◆ PLC program (if applicable)
◆ Parts lists
◆ Other significant items (e.g., manuals for specific process control equipment)

Write workorders to create manuals. Schedule the workorders to maximize the number of equipment pieces covered with a minimum number of workorders. Also, be selective about who you assign to these tasks.

Use existing shop manuals as a starting point for the new manuals. Identify what information you are missing and request these items from the original equipment manufacturer. Also, be prepared to create troubleshooting guides on your own, but be selective about those pieces of equipment you choose.

Once the manuals are created, then check each manual for completeness and accuracy.

Keep all the information in a master library and make shop copies for use on the floor. Consider putting the manuals in binders of a standardized color for easy identification (e.g., one color for the master manuals and another color for the shop copies). Finally, create semiannual PM workorders to check the manuals for completeness and condition. Use the workorder process to perform required manual updates.

SETTING UP INVENTORY

*My kingdom for a nineteen-
millimeter snap ring.*

Once you begin the workorder scheduling process, whether or not you have any control over your inventory will become readily apparent. Let's make it short and sweet: The best maintenance system only works as well as the parts inventory and supply system that supports it.

You will walk a fine line with your parts inventory—having enough, having too much, or having nothing at all. As you set up your inventory, you should keep these thoughts in the back of your mind:

◆ Costs (i.e., what is the inventory holding cost versus purchasing the parts as needed?)

◆ Uptime requirements (i.e., can you afford to be down while you get the needed parts?)

◆ Parts accessibility (i.e., are you located in a large
   city with vendors down the street, or are you located in a small town six hours from a major air-
   port?)

A Quick Review of Inventory Management

The inventory management process begins by having a
clear understanding of why you have parts stored on-site:
to quickly fix equipment. Always remember that equipment downtime and parts inventories both cost the company money. Your job is to determine which is cheaper.
Sounds simple, doesn't it?!

Regardless of the trade-offs, here are the basics of inventory management:

◆ You require spare parts to repair your equipment.
◆ You determine what you need to stock in-house to
   maintain acceptable uptime.
◆ You use these spare parts, then you buy more.
◆ You keep enough stock in the inventory to always
   have the necessary repair parts.

While conceptually simple, building and maintaining the
spare parts inventory can be more difficult than implementing the entire PM system. The difficulties in implementation stem from all the decisions you need to make,
the requirement to track the parts, the cost of the process,
and the nagging fears and questioning: "Am I stocking
the right parts?" My response to these concerns, like
everywhere else in this book, is simple: Just do it! All the
worry, and procrastination, won't help.

In Chapter 1, I advised you to assess if you need a computerized maintenance management system (CMMS). One of the major reasons for having a computerized system is the parts inventory. The computer does a much better job of tracking parts. Most programs are capable of:

◆ Generating parts reorder lists

◆ Creating and tracking purchase orders

◆ Maintaining parts inventory lists

◆ Maintaining a current vendor list

Best of all, the program will do these tasks ten times quicker than any person with a manual system can. A CMMS with automatic report generation capabilities will eliminate busywork and let people spend their time managing the inventory.

However, to be effective, a computerized maintenance program has to be maintained and kept up to date. Do not expect:

◆ Reorder reports to be accurate if you do not relieve the inventory of parts used

◆ The inventory listing to be correct if you do not change locations in the system when you move a part

◆ Purchase orders to be correct if you do not keep the purchasing files up to date

INVENTORY MANAGEMENT STEPS

Just like the PM system, you develop the inventory one step at a time. Once again, you need to get your team involved in the process. To accomplish this task, follow these steps:

1   Sort and organize the existing parts.
2   Determine additional inventory requirements.
3   Develop a purchasing plan for additional inventory items.
4   Develop a reordering plan for the inventory.
5   Maintain the new inventory.

STEP 1: SORT AND ORGANIZE THE EXISTING PARTS

Inventory management begins by sorting and organizing your existing stock. As part of this process, throw out all the broken and obsolete parts.

When organizing your inventory, group all the like parts together and leave room for the parts you plan to add. Try to group parts by some reasonable logic (e.g., brand, size, or machines). Don't get hung up on your organization scheme since you will probably reorganize the inventory one or two more times before you are completely satisfied with the inventory's setup. At this stage you have a basic goal: figuring out what parts you have.

HELPFUL TIP 1

Before you start wholesale disposal of obsolete parts, check if any other plants in your company need those items. Also check if these parts have any resale value on the open market. Remember, one person's junk is another person's treasure!

HELPFUL TIP 2

If you want to manage the inventory with a computerized maintenance management system, then you need to have

a numbering system. The computer program will have its own numbering system structure and it will require you to develop your inventory numbering system within these constraints. When you set out to create a numbering system, be flexible and tailor your numbering system to handle certain realities:

◆ Be advised that mechanical parts (e.g., gears, bearings, seals) will be numbered different from your electrical components (e.g., photoeyes, proximity switches).

◆ Although every vendor has the "same" 6205 bearing, not all vendors have the same retroreflective photoeye—there may be a different mounting base, polarity, or cabling connectors.

Once you have sorted the existing inventory, then it is time to assess how you want to store spare parts. Do you want to stack them on shelves (like the grocery store), put them in cardboard or plastic bins on shelves (as shown in Figure 7-1), or use high tech modular drawer organizer cabinets (shown in Figure 7-2)? The answer to this question lies in how you will maintain and track the parts.

From my own experience, I recommend placing the parts in bins on shelves. This will make visual management easier and you're less likely to have mixed parts. However, if you absolutely have to have the modular drawer cabinets (because they look attractive and give the illusion of true organization), then you should plan on hiring storeroom attendants to keep them maintained. The drawers do not stay organized with an army of technicians rifling through them daily. The modular cabinets, shown in Figure 7-2, work fine when managed by a pro-

Figure 7-1. Plastic bins for storing spare parts.

Figure 7-2. Modular cabinets storage.

fessional inventory staff, such as the staff at your parts vendor's warehouse.

HELPFUL TIP 3

If available floor space is limited, consider installing a mezzanine to expand your parts storage area—but make sure you have sufficient building height to accommodate this solution.

Figure 7-3 shows a mezzanine that one company installed over the maintenance area to store spare parts. Note, however, that this building has twenty-four-foot ceilings that easily accommodate the mezzanine.

HELPFUL TIP 4

Consider segregated metal drawers for your fastener storage. The drawers serve as an efficient way of keeping the

Figure 7-3. A mezzanine can be installed to provide additional parts storage space.

nuts, bolts, and screws separated while making resupply simpler. Make sure you put labels on the front of each drawer to reduce search time. Also, segregate fastener types into sections and sort by size within these sections. Figure 7-4 shows an example of this type of storage solution.

STEP 2: DETERMINE ADDITIONAL INVENTORY REQUIREMENTS

Once you have completed your cleanup, then ask the question: Are these the right parts? If you have 95 percent uptime, are not paying a fortune in overnight freight charges, and aren't calling a parts vendor every night after 10 P.M., then you can truly say you have the right type and quantity of parts. Congratulations—take the rest of the day off!

Figure 7-4. Segregated drawers make excellent storage for nuts, bolts, and screws.

For those of you who aren't able to take the day off, I know what you are thinking: How do you begin adding the "right" parts to the inventory? You improve your inventory in two phases:

◆ Determine what you need (which is step 2).

◆ Develop a purchasing plan to add additional inventory items (which is step 3).

To determine your needs, use in-house purchasing people and vendors. Ask your purchasing staff for a list of those items they "always" buy or the names of the vendors they always frantically call. If your company has a computerized purchasing system, then it can generate a usage report.

Call the vendors on purchasing's list (as well as any others you think are important) and ask these vendors for a printout of your purchases for the last year. Also, ask for a list of items they have overnighted or rushed in the same period. Use this information to determine what you need to add to the existing inventory.

HELPFUL TIP 5

If any vendors cannot readily give you information about your purchases for the past year, then you need to determine if you are using the right vendor! My advice: Unless they are the only source within 500 miles, change vendors immediately. Do not be confused or misguided—those homegrown, garage-size parts houses cost you money in downtime, expedited freight charges, and higher parts charges.

Additionally, if you have not alienated your parts sales representatives with childish or moronic behavior, then you can probably also get them to review the list and make recommendations. In truth, most sales reps want the opportunity to set up a stocking relationship with your company. They would rather sell to you in the daylight than at midnight. Also, all salespeople worth their salt know that they can increase their sales opportunities by building a personal relationship with you. Furthermore, they know that the help they provide you today will build a ton of goodwill and friendship later on, when you move on to bigger and better challenges.

HELPFUL TIP 6

If your vendors don't have a long history with your plant, ask them to perform an equipment survey. This survey will match your repair part requirements to the products they sell. With this information, you can make decisions on what you need to stock because you will have data on the quantity of like parts you have in your plant. Bear in mind these realities, though:

◆ Whenever you request vendors to perform a survey, they have expectations of future orders. Be ethical and use this tip appropriately.

◆ If you have requested the survey, then use their data to purchase parts from them.

◆ On the flip side, many vendors will offer to perform the survey as a way to generate future business. In this situation, you are not under any implied obligation to buy.

HELPFUL TIP 7

To simplify your inventory structure, identify everyday-use items (e.g., nuts, bolts, gloves, caulk) and treat them as expendables. Set them up in easy-access cabinets and use a kanban system to maintain the stocking levels. Figure 7-5 shows a typical expendables cabinet with the reorder list on the door. In addition:

◆ If you have a large enough list of expendables, consider sourcing all these items to one vendor and having the vendor maintain the stock for you.

◆ If you do not have a large enough expendables list, then you can still source these items, except you will have to maintain the stock. Work with the vendor to set up a standard reorder list that you can fill in and fax to the vendor.

◆ If you check with the purchasing people, you may find that setting up a sole source for expendables items is an excellent opportunity for them to establish a proto-

Figure 7-5. Expendables cabinet, with reorder list posted on the door, reduces the time spent searching for everyday supplies.

type electronic ordering project. Figure 7-6 shows a barcode label used by a company that has set up such a system with a major national MRO supplier. The barcode allows personnel to use a handheld scanner to create their replenishment orders for expendable supplies.

STEP 3: DEVELOP A PURCHASING PLAN FOR ADDITIONAL INVENTORY ITEMS

Once you have the vendor recommendations, then you must be the final judge on what you buy. Only you and your staff know what your plant truly needs. Take the sales recommendations and make some decisions.

Once you make the stocking decisions, then you need to determine the purchase timeframes and quantities. Additionally, you must set up the reordering process.

Figure 7-6. Adding barcodes to the bin labels allows implementation of an electronic ordering system.

To set up your purchasing timeframe, start by looking at your parts budget to determine what you can afford to order. Bring your plant manager and accountant into the loop to get their support and advice on how to stock the parts inventory. Make sure that they understand that the purchase list came from analyzing your needs, not a wish list.

Be prepared not to get support. If you find that they do not support the plan, then consider postponing the purchase or making smaller quantity buys over a longer period of time. Look for creative ways to add stock, such as consignment of parts or creation of capitalized spares. Carefully analyze any proposals—but make sure you can hold your end of the deal and you are not paying more in the long run. Finally, remember that you have an annual budget, so next year you get to develop another budget that can include money for a larger parts inventory.

Step 4: Develop a Reordering Plan for the Inventory

Once you get past purchasing the additional inventory, then the real fun begins. Most managed inventories fall into disarray because no plan exists to maintain the stock. At this point, a computerized maintenance management system becomes very handy. If you do not have a CMMS, then you can always use a visual system, kanban, or card system to track the inventory manually.

If you have a computerized inventory system, follow the program's setup instructions for loading your inventory into the system. Review the instructions and develop a plan for entering data. Address what program fields you want/need for your inventory. Also, decide if you want to gather and complete all the data fields at once or just start with the basics and add descriptive data as the system evolves. If you are starting from scratch with a managed inventory, I recommend starting with the basics—part name, part number, vendor, and max/min quantities. Leave the higher-order software functions until later. Look upon these items as opportunities for continuous improvement.

HELPFUL TIP 8

While deciding how you want to maintain your parts, look at the available management reports from your computerized maintenance management system. These reports may give you ideas on how to manage the inventory once you know what is available for use. This review will also help you identify which fields *must* be completed to effectively manage parts with your software program.

Once you have the data loaded into your computer, then run reorder reports daily for a week or two. After this initial period, you'll need only run the report twice weekly.

The reorder report tells you what parts are at minimum stock levels and need to be reordered. You, or your parts person, should review this report and decide what to reorder. In the early stages of the process, look at the reorder report and mentally put each line item into one of the following categories:

◆ The part needs to be reordered.

◆ The part has incorrect max/min levels.

Essentially, by doing this simple mental exercise, you are cleaning up your database. As you find items that fall into the second category, then make changes. Your goal should be to only order routine parts once or twice per week. Ordering once or twice per week will allow you to streamline the process as well as help you leverage your parts pricing with vendors.

Keep a list of parts that you order on an emergency basis. Each time you overnight a part into the plant, make sure the part exists in the database and that the database has the right max/min level. More than likely, you will find out that the part is not in the database and needs to be added.

Once you reach the goal of only ordering parts once or twice per week, then what do you do the rest of the time? Use this time to keep the parts area clean and neat and to look at usage trends.

HELPFUL TIP 9

If you're not using a computerized maintenance management system, set up a card system to maintain the inventory. A card system consists of an index card with the appropriate ordering information placed with the inventory item on the shelf. You reorder the part when the card comes to the front.

You will need to make the same decisions about stocking the part, just as you would if you had a computerized system, except now you will write this information down on the index card. You need part name, vendor, stocking location, price, and max/min information. Additionally, as you order this part over time, write down the dates and quantities ordered on the back of the card to keep a manual purchasing history.

Have the cards preprinted with the desired information. The preprinted card not only looks professional, but also standardizes the way the information is gathered and maintained. Figure 7-7 gives an example of a preprinted inventory card and how to use it. Also, keep in mind that this system is easy in a small operation, but it's murder in a large one.

Always keep a back-up of the information recorded on your inventory index cards. These little index cards have been known to sprout wings!

STEP 5: MAINTAIN THE NEW INVENTORY

This last section sounds redundant. You have gone through all the previous steps, so what is left to maintain? To put it simply, the inventory system dies when:

◆ No one follows the discipline of using the reorder report or the index cards to reorder parts.

◆ No one checks out items or gives the parts person the index cards.

◆ No one keeps the shelves organized.

◆ No one receives parts into the system.

◆ No one places the card back on the shelf with the restocked item.

Bottom line: If you want to have repair parts, then maintain the discipline of the inventory process.

HELPFUL TIP 10

If you have items that you repair and replace in the inventory, then create a "repair warehouse." The repair warehouse allows you to return the item to storage, but does not artificially inflate the carrying cost of your inventory. You only need the repair warehouse if you have a computerized inventory that automatically assigns value to each

Figure 7-7. Example (front and back sides) of a preprinted inventory card.

Front of Card

Part # _____   Vendor: _____

Stocking Location: _____   Phone #: _____

Price: _____

Maximum Qty: _____   Minimum Qty: _____

Alternate Vendor: _____

      Phone #: _____

Back of Card

Reorder History

Qty	Date	Qty	Date
____	____	____	____
____	____	____	____
____	____	____	____
____	____	____	____
____	____	____	____
____	____	____	____

Instructions:

Let's work through a practical example where you stock 6205 bearings:
- You decide to have a minimum of 2 bearings on hand, but no more than 4 in stock at any time.
- You create a card that lists part name, reorder point of 2, and reorder quantity of 2.
- Place this card between the 2nd and 3rd bearing.
- When the 2nd bearing gets removed from the inventory, then the technician takes the card and turns it in to the parts buyer.
- Once the parts buyer receives the card, he orders replacement stock.
- When the new parts are received, you put them back on the shelf.

item received into the inventory. The repair warehouse allows you to repair parts while keeping the accountants (who are watching the value of the inventory) happy.

How Do I Add New Parts?

Once you've gone through the steps to get an inventory system up and running, you still have to know how to add new parts to the system. As with everything else, set up a system for requesting the additional items.

First, create a form that asks for part information, cost, and stocking justification to simplify this process. Figure 7-8 is an example of an inventory stocking request form. The form allows you to maintain an orderly process for adding items to your inventory. It requests not only technical information, but also justification for adding the part. When making these stocking decisions, determine what you need and use the same justification from step 2 of this chapter to make the decision on adding the requested items. The form also contains a line to record the final decision on whether or not to stock the requested item and the signature of the decision maker. Now anyone who wants to add an item can fill out and submit the card. You then periodically review the requests and decide which ones to add.

What About Items That Never Get Used?

If you have a computerized system, then you should be able to run an obsolete parts report that lists the items

Figure 7-8. Inventory stocking form.

Inventory Stocking Request

Requester's Name: _____   Date: _____

Part Name/Number: _____

Vendor: _____   Phone No: _____

Equipment Requiring This Part: _____

_____

Reason for Stocking:_____

_____

Additional Information: _____

Approved/Disapproved   _____

                              Sign and Date

that have not been checked out of the inventory for some period of time (typically one year). Review this report and determine why these parts were not used. For example:

◆ Is it the wrong part?

◆ Has the machine been scrapped?

◆ Was the machine moved to another plant?

◆ Is it a specialized part used once every five years?

Once you have determined why the item has not moved, then act accordingly—get rid of it or keep it.

With the manual card system, this task becomes a lot harder. In fact, unless you have someone with absolutely nothing to do and can go through all the cards on the shelf, then don't bother. (Actually, a good parts person who maintains the shelves will see the items that do not move and take action.)

How Will Inventory Management Improve Uptime?

Obviously, uptime improves when you have the right parts to make quicker repairs. However, uptime will also improve when you start looking at the usage levels of the parts stocked and issue project workorders for usage levels that appear excessive (in quantity and dollars). When examining usage levels, ask these questions:

◆ Why do we use so many of these parts?

◆ Is usage spread across all the machines or just one?

◆ Does the same failure mode always occur?

◆ Could a better quality or differently designed part be used as a replacement?

Answers to these questions will determine if the problem lies in the part, the basic machine design, or just one machine. Once you make this determination, then you know the path of action: Call the part vendor, call the machine vendor, or write a workorder.

SUMMARY

Once you have the workorder system running, then it's time to work on the spare parts inventory. Follow these five steps to establish a managed inventory:

1   Sort and organize the existing parts.

2   Determine additional inventory requirements.

3   Develop a purchasing plan for additional inventory items.

4   Develop a reordering plan for the inventory.

5   Maintain the new inventory.

Your vendors can be indispensable in this process by providing recommendations based on your past buying history. Just remember that the vendor makes recommendations—you make decisions.

Use a system to manage the inventory—a computerized program or a manual card system. With the full range of commercially available computerized maintenance management systems and low-priced computers, I recommend going with a CMMS. Managing the inventory means setting up a plan to restock parts at some predetermined quantity and sticking with the process. You also need to set up a system to add parts to the inventory and to look at obsolete items. Finally, once you get all these activities completed, then start to look at those items with high usages to determine where uptime improvements can be made either through the use of different parts or machine modifications.

8

MAINTAINING THE SYSTEM

✓

*What am I going to do with all
my spare time?*

Well, we've put the systems in place. What's left—declare total victory, put on our rose-colored glasses, and sit by the pool in blissful happiness? Wrong! Now we have to maintain it or (even better) improve it.

You need to treat your new system like your child. It requires continued care, feeding, and guidance. You need to:

◆ Keep the scheduling process going.

◆ Ensure the workorders get completed at acceptable quality levels.

◆ Ensure the PM workorders remain current.

◆ Keep ordering parts.

◆ Look for opportunities to improve the process.

Why Does the World's Greatest Maintenance Management System Fail?

What's the single biggest cause for failure of PM systems? It's when you stop scheduling the workorders! How could this happen? People usually stop scheduling because they fall back into their old habits: They get too busy, no one turns in workorders, or no one follows up on parts.

So what's the magic answer for keeping the system alive? Schedule. Schedule. Schedule. The daily schedule keeps the program running. It is the vehicle for getting the work done.

Daily scheduling is like exercise. If you keep doing it day in and day out, it becomes a habit and it gets easier. Also, remember that not every schedule you plan has to be a masterpiece of efficiency and perfection.

As for the problem of people not turning in workorders, this is a totally different situation. One of the main reasons people stop writing workorders is they find out that you will do it for them. Resist the urge to be a nice guy and be their secretary. This is an area where you need to get the help of your boss. Bosses need to let the rest of the plant know that they support the workorder system. They also need to learn a new response when someone complains about not getting something done: "Did you write a workorder?"

People also stop writing workorders when they perceive that nothing is happening with their request. Once again, you need to stay on top of the workorders being submitted and being scheduled. When a technician completes the workorder, then close it out.

Don't just inform the workorder's originator that the workorder is done. Instead, ask the individual to sign the workorder and "accept" the work as complete. However, do not let this step become an efficiency trap. Some of your technicians might use this sign-off process as a method for avoiding work. I've seen technicians literally spend hours chasing signatures. Avoid this trap by closing the workorder and then using the plant's mail system to return workorders for signature. If those making the workorder request do not agree that the work is complete, then they can send the workorder back with their comments. This process keeps the paper flowing and lets people know that their request is complete.

HELPFUL TIP 1

Start an "Open Workorder Report" to keep people informed of the status of their workorder. This report does not need to be elaborate; at minimum it should include the workorder number, name of requester, date of origination, topic, and comments. Send the list out periodically (I suggest weekly) and you will eliminate calls about workorders.

A note of caution: Once you start sending this report out, then you must make the commitment to keep moving the workorders through the system. If you do not manage the workorders, then everybody knows because you told them in the report!

HELPFUL TIP 2

If you purchase a computerized maintenance management system (CMMS), then make sure it can generate an

Open Workorder Report as part of its "canned" management reports. If the program has such a report already set up, then you can automatically generate the report weekly and send it out.

HELPFUL TIP 3

Make your basic workorder form a carbonless two-part form so the originator can keep the copy for their records. If you lose someone's workorder, then you can get a copy from them. In the never-ending world of office politics, if you stay on top of your workorders, the two-part form can be a useful tool for communication—but it can also be used as a powerful weapon against you if you do not manage the workorders! Any of the workorders in Appendix 4 will lend themselves to being used as two-part forms.

MAINTAINING YOUR QUALITY LEVEL

If you can keep the workorders going, then make sure you also keep them going with quality. The last thing you want for yourself and your department is the reputation for performing poor work. To avoid this problem, periodically check on the work in progress during your day. Make sure the work being done meets your standards. If the work does not meet your standards, then have it corrected. Also make sure that your technicians know your expectations so you avoid finding work that requires corrections.

In addition, consider scheduling periodic quality audits

of PM workorders by yourself or your supervisors. This quality audit ensures that procedures are being followed and that the technicians understand the PM process. The audit is also a good way to catch anyone who is "pencil whipping" the PM workorders.

Figure 8-1 shows a form for conducting PM quality audits. The form asks for an evaluation of both the work-

Figure 8-1. A quality assurance form for conducting PM audits.

ABC **Company**	Preventive Maintenance Quality Assurance Review		Date: _____

Technician Reviewed: _____   Reviewer: _____
Clock No: _____

PM Workorder Reviewed: _____

Workorder   Equipment
No: _____   Interval: _____   No: _____

Time Work   Time Work
Started _____   Completed: _____

Workorder Quality:	Circle one:	
Were all safety procedures followed?	Y	N
Did technician have all required tools?	Y	N
Did workorder provide sufficient information?		
logic flow?	Y	N
required parts?	Y	N
timing and alignment?	Y	N

Please provide additional information on all NO answers and recommended changes:

_____
_____
_____
_____

Technician Performance:	Circle one:	
Demonstrated understanding of safety requirements?	Y	N
Demonstrated understanding of procedure?	Y	N
Any additional training required?	Y	N
Cleaned area upon completion of work?	Y	N

Please provide additional information on all NO answers and required training/improvements:

_____
_____
_____
_____

order and the technician. It asks Yes and No questions and requests additional information for all No answers.

Keeping the PM Workorders Current

After poor workmanship, nothing makes your PM program lose credibility faster than inaccurate or outdated PM workorders. Worse yet, this situation causes doubt to arise from your crew. Therefore, as you make changes to your equipment, make changes to the PMs. Also, as repair parts or lubrication products change, make sure to update the PM workorders accordingly.

Don't be afraid to get your technicians involved in keeping the PM workorders current. Assign them the task of making the corrections they discover as they perform the PMs.

What About Parts?

Once you get the scheduling process working at acceptable quality levels, then you will discover the next roadblock to completing projects is availability of parts. Without parts, projects stop happening and the repairs all become bandages. The lack of parts can turn into a major demoralizing factor.

To keep the parts flowing, keep using your inventory system. If you keep generating reorder reports and ordering the parts on these reports, then you will have the parts necessary to avoid Band-Aid repairs. For project workorders requiring special parts, consider letting technicians find the necessary parts and fill out requisitions. Once you have their completed requisitions, then you can order the parts required to complete the workorder.

MAKING CONTINUOUS IMPROVEMENTS (OR LIKE A SHARK, MOVE FORWARD OR DIE)

Once you can maintain the system, then it is time to think about improvement. What exactly does this mean? It means looking for opportunities to make the operation run smoother. You will find these opportunities by looking at your parts orders for repair trends. What kinds of possible trends are there? As one example, the motor on conveyor line 3 keeps burning up (three times in two months). Or maybe the gearbox oil on the extruders looks clean as a whistle every time we change it during the monthly PM. Or maybe you discover that it takes half the shift to get the Smith casepackers lined out after a changeover. When you see one of these trends, then you should take one of the following actions:

1   Initiate project workorders to correct the problem.

2   Modify the appropriate PM workorder to remedy the problem or take advantage of the situation.

When you start the troubleshooting process to eliminate a newly spotted trend, follow a systematic process to determine the potential causes of the problem. Usually the problem stems either from the:

◆ Equipment

◆ Operating conditions

◆ Operating parameters

Ask questions about the similarities between the equipment that fails and the like pieces of equipment that do not fail. Common questions might be:

◆ Do all these motors have the same failure mode?

◆ Do these bearings run warmer than the others?

◆ How much slower or faster does this unit run than the other units?

◆ Is this part installed properly?

◆ Is this the right model part for this application?

During your investigation, look for comparisons and contrasts to solve your problems. Once you have this information, then you will be on the path to putting this problem to bed.

As an example, look at the fan motor pictured in Figure 8-2. Suppose this variable-speed fan, which exhausts smoke from a gas curing oven, has a history of motor failures every thirty to forty-five days. Also suppose that this fan is part of an oven exhaust system that includes eleven other fans, but none of these fans exhibit the same failure trend. What are the possible causes for these failures? What are the questions you need to ask to resolve this problem?

Follow the process of looking at the variables associated with the problem—namely, the equipment, operating conditions, and operating parameters. Your potential questions might be:

Figure 8-2. What would cause this 1 HP fan to have a high failure rate?

Equipment

◆ Are all the fan units identical?

◆ Are all the motors and drives the same make, model, and voltage?

◆ Where does the exhaust fan sit relative to the other fans (e.g., on the end or in the middle)?

◆ What is the fan's distance from the control panel?

Operating Conditions

◆ Does this exhaust stack discharge warmer air than the other stacks?

◆ Are the exhausted fumes any different from those exhausted by the other fans?

Operating Parameters

◆ Where does the fan's operating RPM fall on the motor's performance curve?

◆ Do all the fans operate at the same speed?

◆ Does any pattern exist relative to time of day, day of the week, or production product?

Once you know the answer to these questions, then you will know which direction to head for problem resolution.

HELPFUL TIP 4

Notice how the maintenance department installed the fan motor in Figure 8-2. They used cords with twist-lock connectors to speed up repairs and to make running repairs possible. Figure 8-3 is a detailed view of the twist-lock connector. As you embark on the path of continuous improvement, look for ways to improve the repair time for equipment. Specifically:

◆ Look for areas where quick disconnects or bypasses make sense and will help in repairs. Adding valves and quick connects can be an expensive proposition, so use these items where a potential payback exists. When you do make these changes, make sure that the plugs, valves, or connectors are properly sized and allowed by the applicable building code.

◆ Be sure to mark any new valves or bypasses so that technicians and operators know their intended use. Nothing hurts your credibility more than to incur downtime or process scrap because someone closed or opened the wrong valve.

Figure 8-3. The use of the twist-lock connector improves maintainability.

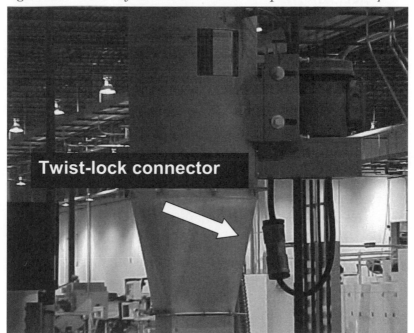

Finally, think about continuous improvement in a very selfish way. The more projects you complete and the better the PM system operates, the fewer surprises and headaches you must deal with. It means you'll get less irate calls, go home earlier and, in general, do more of the things you want to do!

HELPFUL TIP 5

To spot trends, set up separate semiannual or annual reviews with your three or four largest suppliers. During this review, look at the top five to ten items you purchase most from each vendor. Close this review by challenging these vendors to suggest options for reducing these quantities.

HELPFUL TIP 6

As you discover trends and look for ways to improve your maintenance program, assess whether the problem area might best be handled by an outside service. For example, many companies outsource HVAC maintenance to ensure compliance with Environmental Protection Agency rules. Other areas where an outsourcing option might apply include hoist inspections, confined space repairs, fire extinguisher inspections, and sprinkler system inspections.

As you might already suspect, there's no right or wrong answer when it comes to the decision to use outside services. You must make the decision based on your department goals, cost considerations, and whether the outside service's quality meets your expectations.

HELPFUL TIP 7

Use production data to spot trends or identify issues. The scrap and productivity reports should show the equipment-related problems. Here is some additional advice:

◆ Do not take the raw data at face value. You must ask questions and understand the data to make sure you are on the right problem/solution track.

◆ Share information with the people in your department. Ask for their input on why these problems are occurring and what the potential solutions are.

◆ Proceed to solve the problem only after you have the facts and input from your staff. Remember, nothing undermines your credibility more than well-intentioned but misguided continuous improvement projects.

HELPFUL TIP 8

If you identify any equipment requiring routine rebuilds, but you find yourself unable to continually apply resources, then consider outsourcing the rebuild to a local shop. In this situation:

◆ When you send out equipment for rebuild, be selective about who you choose. Make sure the service providers you choose have the resources to do the job, and give them any required tips or training.

◆ If you find the rebuild program helps, then evaluate whether you want to bring the work in-house in six to eight months. You can use the cost data for the outside shop to justify/offset the labor cost.

◆ Be sure to monitor your outside vendors to ensure they stick to the agreed schedule and maintain expected quality levels.

HELPFUL TIP 9

To prevent major building problems, make sure your new PM program includes checks of the electrical panels, roof, and sprinkler system. These inspections are vital because:

◆ An annual infrared (IR) scan of all electrical panels can save major repair dollars and downtime.

◆ Likewise, an annual roof inspection by a trained professional can prevent leaks and deterioration. (Remember, you only find roof problems when it rains or snows—exactly when you can't or shouldn't get up on the roof.)

◆ The importance of a well-maintained sprinkler system

is obvious. When you need it, then you want it to work; but when it fails, it can put out a lot of water.

LEARNING FROM YOUR FAILURES

Always perform an autopsy on the major breakdowns or bad startups. Always conduct this review after the fire has been put out and try to avoid conducting an inquisition. Use the following questions as a starting point to figure out what happened and to determine how to avoid the problem in the future:

◆ What can we do better or different next time?

◆ Can we schedule the crew differently, change the procedure, and perform more frequent checks?

◆ Should we change the widget more frequently?

◆ Should we use a different widget?

When you start to follow this thought process, then you are on the way to having a successful system.

While on the subject of failures, let's discuss the topic of problem startups after major PM overhauls. In the infancy of your PM program, you may encounter problems with startup. This issue can become one of the biggest complaints made by opponents of preventive maintenance systems. They use this situation to put forth the "run it until it breaks" philosophy. These poor misguided souls will claim they could have run the equipment longer and produced more product instead of letting the maintenance guys "play with the equipment." In light of these charges, the best course of action is to "turn the other cheek" and get on with correcting the process so the same mistakes do not happen twice. Be advised, however, that these people will drive the PM program into the ground for you if you continue to have a problem after the major overhauls. Many plant managers find it very convenient to save maintenance cost when they can find a convincing argument.

To avoid poor startups, use planning and preparation. Developing a startup checklist will dramatically increase your chances of success. The checklist should run through:

1 Pre-startup test and checkout requirements (such as testing motors for rotation)

2 All startup steps (actions and equipment settings)

3 All final safety checks to ensure that:
   ◆ Associates are clear of the operating area.
   ◆ All safeties are operational.
   ◆ All guards have been reinstalled.

4 All large or special tools used on the project, to ensure they are removed and accounted for

If you make the decision to develop and use a startup checklist, then treat it as a living document. Continue to update and change the checklist as new issues or information arises.

HELPFUL TIP 10

As you create your startup checklist and related safety checks (or any other type of form recommended throughout this book), consider numbering the forms to help track their evolution. If you work in a facility that has ISO or QS certification, then this tip is a requirement for document control.

In ISO- or QS-certified facilities, work with your local coordinators to make sure you follow the established guidelines for your facility.

MORE ABOUT CMMS PROGRAMS

If you seriously embrace the continuous improvement process, then you will definitely want and need a computerized PM program. Any good software program will let you track the repair history of individual equipment as well as families of equipment. In addition, keep future plans for continuous improvement in mind when you select a computer system. Figure 8-4 suggests questions to consider when evaluating CMMS programs. Be advised that no right or wrong answers exist to these questions—just satisfy yourself that the program meets your needs. Also, don't be intimidated by some of the "techno geeks" or "one-system know-it-alls" who'll try to shoehorn your problems or desires into their solution.

Figure 8-4. Questions to consider when making a CMMS purchase.

◆ How does the program categorize information?

◆ How rigid are the naming conventions?

◆ What flexibility does the CMMS have for report generation?

◆ How adaptable is the program to future plans such as predictive maintenance, reliability-centered maintenance (RCM), or total productive maintenance (TPM)?

Summary

Once you get the system set up, then it becomes time to sustain the gain. You sustain the gain by managing the workorders and keeping the parts stocked.

Preventive maintenance workorders need to be monitored and managed just like troublecall and project workorders. Make sure you schedule them. Also, over time, monitor their effectiveness and make changes as required. Among the potential changes to the workorders will be decreasing intervals, adding additional steps, listing required repair parts, and increasing intervals. (Note: Make sure you have a good handle on your equipment before you start increasing the interval to avoid a potentially expensive learning experience.)

Ask yourself these questions after every surprise breakdown or bad startup:

◆ What can we do better or different next time?
◆ Can we schedule the crew differently, change the procedure, and perform more frequent checks?
◆ Should we change the widget more frequently?
◆ Should we use a different widget?

Apply the same continuous improvement philosophies to the inventory. Look for those items that seem to always be out of stock or experiencing failure. Don't be afraid to ask your vendors for help to improve your inventory.

To restate the bottom line, operating a successful system requires staying on top of the workorders. Continuously look for ways to improve both the PM system and the overall operation. These actions become self-fulfilling prophecies because you continue to solve problems and prevent them from reoccurring. The continuous improvement process also sets the stage for focusing on advanced maintenance practices such as predictive maintenance, reliability-centered maintenance, or total productive maintenance.

TEST TIME

This test consists of two problem-solving scenarios; see Appendix 5 for the answers.

1. You have five process lines that use the belt pull machine shown in Figure 8-5 to move product

Figure 8-5. This machine has excessive belt failures—what questions must you ask to find out why?

through the curing process. Each line has two of these machines and all machines are the same make, model, and age. Write down the questions you would ask if you experienced excessive belt failures under the following three scenarios:

a. Only the machines on one process line experience excessive belt failures (the belt life is 25 percent of all the other lines).

b. Only the first machine on each line experiences excessive belt wear (the belt life is 25 percent of all the other lines).

c. The belt failures occur randomly across all ten machines.

2. You experience frequent circuit-breaker trips for an electrical panel (similar to the one shown in Figure 8-6) that provides power to an office area. The electrical panel on the right regularly trips out in the summer and winter, but not in the spring or fall. The electrical panel on the left does not experience these failures. What questions would you ask to determine a course of action for resolution of this problem?

Figure 8-6. *Electrical panel on right trips prematurely.*

9

PLANNING FOR SUCCESS

✓

No plan is a plan for failure.

In Chapter 1, I asked you to read the entire book before embarking on implementation. I also asked you to begin thinking about what resources you would need for implementing these steps. These resources include both the people you need in the short term to create the PM workorder and inventory as well as the long-term staff to keep the system running.

While you were thinking about the resources you will require, hopefully you also thought about how long the process would take to complete. If you have thought about timing, then you have probably begun to assess the size of your plant and the uniqueness of your equipment.

By addressing resources and timing, you effectively bound the problem of implementing professional maintenance management. I propose that you use the answers to the resource and timing questions to build an implementation roadmap.

The roadmap, or plan, will guide your journey toward professional maintenance management and help you track plan execution. The roadmap is essential for explaining the program to both your boss and your associates.

Who Will Build the PMs and the Inventory?

Let us address the short-term resource requirement first since it is the easiest problem to address. In the short term, you have the most flexibility to move and reassign people. Therefore, in this stage, look at your crew and pick a small team to perform the implementation process. When picking your implementation team, choose individuals with:

◆ Equipment knowledge

◆ Reading and writing abilities

◆ Team participation skills

◆ Organizational skills

It's vital that you don't underestimate the importance of the last two requirements—team participation skills and organizational abilities—for the selected associates.

Also, when making your assessments and decisions, keep one eye on the future and one eye on the present. Do not forget that someone needs to perform plant maintenance. Therefore, not everyone can be on the team.

If you pass over "stars" because you need them to run the plant, be sensitive to their feelings. (Remember, everybody wants to be part of the latest hot thing!) Be upfront—tell them why you made this decision and that you are counting on their support to keep the place running.

HELPFUL TIP 1

Don't be boxed into thinking that only team members can create equipment lists and PM workorders. Use all available resources and opportunities to get things done. If you've passed over some of your best people because you need them to run the plant, you can still have them participate by asking them to review the drafts of the building breakdown, the equipment list, PM workorders, and inventory additions. By engaging your "stars" in this way you are helping to ensure you get their program buy-in.

HELPFUL TIP 2

Do not forget the need to plan for administrative support. Someone needs to turn this data into workorders.

Even if you do not have a computerized maintenance management program, you still need to put the information into a typed format. With spare clerical support in short supply in most organizations, consider hiring temporary help to get the information typed up.

Save the final decision on administrative resources until you have reviewed the plan with your boss. Your boss may have suggestions for resources that you did not think of or thought were off-limits.

WHAT ABOUT THE LONG-TERM RESOURCES?

Most people avoid the long-term resource question. They hope that the problem never shows up or that the issue will be magically solved. There's even a small group that plans on seeking forgiveness later when it becomes apparent that additional people are required and the organization has to provide support.

I recommend that you look this issue squarely in the eye and make decisions. Ignoring the question of who will run the system only postpones the final outcome. If you need additional people, then address the issue with your boss and the human resources department. Don't expect immediate approval, and be prepared to justify your request.

Determining how you will maintain the system boils down to two very simple questions:

◆ Who will schedule workorders?

◆ Who will order parts?

Before you can answer these questions, though, you need to ask some more:

◆ Who do you have available?

◆ What is your own available time?

◆ How much time will be required to perform these jobs?

◆ How much time will be freed up by the implementation of a maintenance management system?

When you look at who is available, be sensitive to the human resources issues that can pop up. Issues such as service time and past work history can get in the way of the right decision if the decision is not properly coordinated.

After you decide who will schedule workorders and order parts, then make sure to include them on the implementation team. You may even want these people to lead the team.

One final note on the long-term resources for managing this program. Realistically assess your needs. Don't hire more people, or create new positions, if you have the time to do these activities yourself. On the other hand, if you have a large plant or multiple plants, do not mislead yourself into believing that you can manage everything yourself. (Never forget that there are many unemployed people with a superman complex.)

HELPFUL TIP 3

Don't overlook hourly associates as potential candidates to schedule workorders and order parts. By assigning these positions to hourly associates, you may create a more workable solution for your boss and the human resources department.

If you determine you do not have any in-house candidates, then consult the HR department on options to fill your needs.

HOW LONG WILL THIS TAKE? I'M IN A HURRY!

Once you have identified the "who," then it is time to identify the "how" and the "when." Start this process by gathering your team and discussing the steps required to implement the program.

Realistically discuss how long the various phases of the program will take to accomplish. Specific discussion topics should include:

◆ How long will it take to implement workorder scheduling?

◆ How long will it take to develop the equipment list?

◆ How many more items will need to be added to the book's generic equipment list?

◆ How long will it take to write PM workorders?

◆ How many common equipment types and groups exist within the plant?

◆ How much coordination time will be required for equipment lists and PM workorders?

◆ When do we start work on the inventory?

Take the team's answers to these questions and create a schedule. To keep the project focused, set up an "action plan" schedule in increments of days and weeks. Figure 9-1 shows a draft schedule plan for an average-size plant named ABC Factory in the example.

When making the schedule, allow plenty of time for coordination activities. Also, don't forget that someone will have to type the PM workorder and inventory information. Therefore, to avoid potential schedule slips, include these events as part of the program's implementation schedule.

HELPFUL TIP 4

If a scheduled activity lasts longer than one week, then schedule periodic reviews. These reviews should assess schedule status and program workorder status.

Use the PM workorder development master list (discussed in Chapter 5) to track progress.

Figure 9-1. Sample action plan/schedule.

Action Plan: Implementation Plan for ABC Factory

Start
Date: 1-Mar

Champion: _____ John Gross

Action Steps	Who:	Weeks
Develop plan & select team	Gross	1
Coordinate plan	Gross	1
Implement scheduling		
Set up files	Smith	1/2
Sort and schedule workorders	Smith	1/2
Begin scheduling	Smith	2
Define logical parts	Team	1
Build equipment list		
Modify generic equipment list	Team	1
Develop 1st draft of list	Team	2
Edit list	Smith	1/2
Finalize list	Team	1/2
Write PM workorders		
Write PM workorders	Team	4
Edit and schedule	Smith	2
Send out 1st draft of workorders	Smith	1
Build manuals	Team	3
Inventory management		
Sort current inventory	Wilson	2
Determine additional inventory items	Gross/Wilson	2
Develop purchasing plan	Gross	1/2
Develop reordering plan	Wilson	1/2
Begin weekly trend reviews	Gross/Smith/Wilson	

(Gantt chart weeks 1–40; % Complete 20 40 60 80 100)

HELPFUL TIP 5

The schedule format shown in Figure 9-1 will also work for other projects. If you need to develop a quick and easy-to-use schedule for other projects, then consider using this same format. (Appendix 4 contains a blank copy of the action plan form for your use.)

When you have completed your schedule, then start the coordination process. Begin the coordination process with your implementation team. Make sure the team agrees with the schedule and that it reflects the group discussions held before building the schedule. Once the team agrees on the schedule, then it is time to discuss the schedule with your boss.

When discussing the schedule with your boss, I suggest presenting the schedule with a written summary, such as the draft summary in Figure 9-2. The summary should include:

- Description of the proposed program's scope
- Team member names
- Significant project issues (e.g., clerical support, computerized PM program purchase, or labor concerns)
- Required long-term resources
- Potential payback

HELPFUL TIP 6

Do not develop your plans in a vacuum. Just as you need a team to successfully implement the program, you need your boss's support. To that end:

Figure 9-2. Summary of a PM program implementation plan.

Maintenance Management System

Implementation Plan

Scope:

> This project will implement a seven-step plan that will establish a scheduling system, preventive maintenance plan, and a managed inventory. The attached schedule shows the steps and the schedule for implementing the program.

Team Members:

> Jack Wilson, William Ryan, Bob Smith, Harvey Carlson

Significant Issues:

- Additional resources required to manage the system after completion of the implementation phase:
  - □ Parts clerk and administrative clerk required

- Computerized maintenance program required to manage the program:
  - □ Approximately 200 pieces of equipment to be covered
  - □ Current inventory value estimated at $500,000

- Expect to add spare parts to the inventory over time:
  - □ No estimate of cost
  - □ Overnight and premium freight charges averaging $3,000/month

Potential Payback:

Decrease plant scrap by 3%, which will save $25,000/month

◆ **Discuss your plans to form a team and to implement the seven-step process with your boss before forming the implementation team.**

◆ **Give your bosses a copy of this book so they understand how you will implement the program.**

HELPFUL TIP 7

Create an information board for sharing the schedule and pertinent information to keep everyone informed of the project's progress. Use this board to post the draft documents such as the equipment lists.

After you have completed the coordination process with your boss, then coordinate the plan with your crew. Review both the schedule and implementation issues with them. I also recommend that you stress to the staff that this is a long-term project and not a fad-of-the-month activity. Expect questions and concerns from those people who were not in the original planning group.

Once you have completed the work of coordination, get started implementing the seven steps to professional maintenance management! As you progress through the various steps, keep the schedule updated. If a task gets delayed, make sure you understand what happened. Finally, share these updates so that everyone knows the program's status.

SUMMARY

Before starting to implement the steps in this program, build an implementation roadmap or plan. This roadmap should address the short-term and long-term resources you need, as well as the timing to implement each of the seven steps.

Be open and honest with yourself and your management about the expected resource requirements. Make sure you develop the schedule with the members of the implementation team. Also, do not forget to schedule time for administrative activities and for coordination of the equipment lists and PM workorders.

Once you have completed the plan, coordinate it with the implementation team, your boss, and your crew. Remember that coordination will go easier if you keep everyone in the loop as you develop the roadmap.

When you complete coordination of the plan, then start implementing. As you progress down the implementation path, keep the schedule updated and keep everyone informed of the project's progress. Consider developing an information board to post relevant information on the project.

10

CONCLUSION

✓

*It's time to set sail
on the journey!*

Hopefully by now you have begun to see how the seven steps will work for you. Follow these steps in order and make sure to complete one step before moving on to the next:

1   Establish scheduling.
2   Break down the facilities into logical parts.
3   Develop an equipment list and assign equipment numbers.
4   Develop and issue preventive maintenance instructions (PMs).
5   Locate and/or develop equipment manuals.
6   Develop a managed inventory.
7   Monitor the program's effectiveness and make improvements.

Do not underestimate the need to complete the preparatory work before starting to write PM workorders. Additionally, the implementation process works best when you work with a team.

Throughout the book I have recommended that you purchase a CMMS program. I have also recommended that you carefully make this decision and select a program that meets the needs of your organization. Select the CMMS program that lets you manage your maintenance operation the way you want to manage it. Use the advice offered throughout the book to guide your decision.

As you move through the implementation process, I hope you begin to see professional maintenance management not as a one-time project, but rather as a never-ending journey. The system that you implement needs to be continually improved based on new events, new information, or new technology. Use the updating recommendations in this book to integrate changes into your system. If you make significant changes, then don't be afraid to start all over from scratch.

In conclusion, good luck with developing a maintenance management program. It takes time and hard work to develop a successful program, but the rewards will be worth it, both to your organization and to yourself.

Thank you for your time.

APPENDIX 1
ABBREVIATIONS LIST

CMMS	Computerized maintenance management system
Ft	Foot
HP	Horsepower
HVAC	Heating, ventilation, and air-conditioning
I/O	Input/output
IR	Infrared
ISO	International Standards Organization
LAN	Local area network
No	Number
PC	Personal computer
PLC	Programmable Logic Controller
PM	Preventive maintenance
QS	Quality Systems
RCM	Reliability-centered maintenance
ROP	Reorder point
ROQ	Reorder quantity
RPM	Revolutions per minute
S/N	Serial number
TPM	Total productive maintenance

TPW   Total productive work
WAN   Wide area network

APPENDIX 2
GENERIC EQUIPMENT LIST

Use the following generic equipment list as the starting point for your plant's equipment list. This list uses six to seven digits to specify equipment. The first three digits (**XXX**-XXXX) represent common *equipment types*, such as boilers or curing ovens or air-handling units. The last three or four digits (XXX-**XXXX**) represent sequentially numbered *pieces of equipment*. This numbering method provides a simple way of categorizing your equipment and can be easily communicated. It also allows you to develop equipment trends and should help during data entry when setting up your computerized PM system.

The numbering system attempts to name and number common equipment while setting up a structure for naming and numbering process-specific equipment. The proposed structure for equipment types is:

1XX	Building Equipment
2XX	Generic Process Equipment
3XX–9XX	Process-Specific Equipment

155

To explain how to use this system, I'll use "air-handling units" as an example. In the proposed generic building equipment list, 165 represents air-handling units. Therefore a plant's air-handling units would be numbered 165-001, 165-002, and on through 165-999. Please note that not all the pieces of equipment grouped in one type have to have the same basic name: For example, 165-001 might be an "office air handler" and 165-009 might be a "maintenance shop fresh air handler." (They also don't have to be the same make or model.)

Reserve 300–900 for process-specific items. To use these numbers, identify the equipment in the process and establish numbers for each type of equipment. Next, number each piece of equipment sequentially by type, just like in the air-handling unit example. Refer back to Chapter 4 for additional information on developing process-specific equipment numbers.

In addition, consider these Helpful Tips:

Helpful Tip 1. Don't fall into the trap of thinking that every process line needs its own three- or four-digit number for each piece of equipment. Develop the numbers based on the equipment's function rather than make or model.

Helpful Tip 2. If you have more than six process areas, then add a digit to the type category. Under these conditions, the equipment number changes from XXX-XXXX to **X**XXX-XXXX. However, before taking this step, analyze whether you truly have too many process areas or have failed to categorize equipment types properly.

Building Equipment List (1XX)

Number	Description
	Building General
101	Building, Computer Room
102	Building, Exterior
103	Building, Lunchroom
104	Building, Office
105	Building, Restroom
106	Building, Telephone Room
107	Chemical Storage
108	Compactor
109	Elevator
110	Hazardous Waste Storage
111	Roof, General
112-125	Building, *Insert Name of Common Area*

Number	Description
	Building Plumbing
150	Main, Water
151	Aerator
152	Chlorination System
153	Reverse Osmosis System
154	Well Pump
155	Water Fountains
156	Water Tower
157	Water Treatment
158	Water Meter
159	Sewer Flow Meter
160-164	*Additional Items*

Number	Description
	Electrical
130	Electrical Room, General
131	Main, Electrical
132	Distribution Panel (DP)
133	Remote Panel (RP)
134	Generator
135	Intercom System
136	Lights, Exterior
137	Lights, Interior
138	Motor Control Center
139	Switchgear
140	Telephone System
141	Transformer
142	Local Area Network (LAN)
143	Wide Area Network (WAN)
144-149	*Additional Items*

Number	Description
	HVAC
165	Air-Handling Unit
166	Chiller, HVAC
167	Boiler, HVAC
168	Fan
169	Cooling Tower, HVAC
170	Thermostat
171	Air Conditioner
172	Air Makeup Unit
173-179	*Additional Items*

Building Equipment List (1XX) - Continued

Number   Description

Emergency System

Number	Description
180	Alarm System
181	Fire Door
182	Fire Pump
183	Fire Pump Room, General
184	Fire Vent
185	Post Indicator Valves (PIV)
186	Sprinkler Inspector's Test Point
187	Sprinkler Riser
188	Sprinkler System
189	Lights, Emergency
190	Eye Wash
191-199	*Additional Items*

Generic Process Equipment List (2XX)

Number	Description	Number	Description
	Maintenance General		**Warehouse**
201	Tool, Hand	235	Forklift
202	Tool, Power	236	Pallet Jack
203	Cutting Torch	237	Lights, Dock Doors
204	Welder	238	Dock Locks
205	Saw	239	Dock Levelers
206	Mill	240	Battery-Charging Room, General
207	Lathe	241	Battery Charger
208	Parts Washer	242	Battery Changer
209	Ladder	243	Battery Hoisting Bar
210	Safety Harness	244	Stretch Wrapper
211	Lift, Manual	245	Scale
212	Lift, Powered	246-254	*Additional Items*
213-219	*Additional Items*		

Number	Description	Number	Description
	Compressed Air		**Process Heating and Cooling**
220	Compressor Room, General	255	"Boiler Room," General
221	Compressor	256	Boiler
222	Air Dryer	257	Chiller
223	Tank, Air Receiver	258	Cooling Tower
224	Air Management System	259	Circulating Pumps
225	Condensate Drain Device	260	Heat Exchanger
226	Valve, Pressure Relief	261	Tank, Makeup Water
227	Oil Separator	262-269	*Additional Items*
228-234	*Additional Items*		

Number   **Description**

Process General

270	Conveyor
271	Crane
272	Vacuum Pump
273	Blower
274	Baghouse
275	Dust Collector
276	Sifter
277	Cyclone
278	Hoist, Manual
279	Hoist, Powered
280-299	*Additional Items*

APPENDIX 3
PM PROCEDURE WORKSHEET

GENERAL GUIDANCE

Use the following worksheets to develop your PM workorders for each piece of equipment. The sheets have been set up to create the workorders by intervals (e.g., daily, weekly, biweekly, monthly, bimonthly, quarterly, semiannually, and annually) and operating and non-operating procedures.

Do not forget safety procedures when completing the workorders. Be as specific as possible on steps and required settings and parts.

Do not be afraid of the length of the sheet. Use all the pages that apply. Also, realize that these sheets represent the same sequence of workorders used to conduct the PM program.

PM Procedure Worksheet

Name: _____   Equipment Number: _____

Date: _____   Equipment Name: _____

Instructions:
List all required maintenance procedures by interval (e.g., weekly, every other week, monthly, bimonthly, quarterly, semi-annually, annually). Use separate sheets for each interval as required (i.e., you may not have any procedures for some intervals, such as every other week or bimonthly). List both operating and nonoperating procedures. Identify all required safety procedures. Attach additional sheets, if necessary.

Use every resource available for completing this worksheet, including:
- Personal knowledge
- Equipment manuals
- Other technicians, supervisors, operators, etc.

List any unique safety precautions, such as multiple sources of power, etc.:

1 _____
2 _____
3 _____

List estimated required time to perform each procedure. Complete this section after completing the

Weekly	_____	Bimonthly	_____
Every other week	_____	Quarter	_____
Monthly	_____	Semiannual	_____
		Annual	_____

Daily PM Procedure

List all special tools required for these procedures:

1 _____   4 _____
2 _____   5 _____
3 _____   6 _____

List all supplies required to perform these procedures by interval:

1 _____   4 _____
2 _____   5 _____
3 _____   6 _____

Equipment
Running
 Y or N ?   Procedure:

Weekly PM Procedure

List all special tools required for these procedures:

1 _____ 4 _____
2 _____ 5 _____
3 _____ 6 _____

List all supplies required to perform these procedures by interval:

1 _____ 4 _____
2 _____ 5 _____
3 _____ 6 _____

Equipment
Running
  Y or N ?   Procedure:

Every Other Week PM Procedure

List all special tools required for these procedures:

1   ————————————   4   ————————————
2   ————————————   5   ————————————
3   ————————————   6   ————————————

List all supplies required to perform these procedures by interval:

1   ————————————   4   ————————————
2   ————————————   5   ————————————
3   ————————————   6   ————————————

Equipment
Running
  Y or N ?   Procedure:

Monthly PM Procedure

List all special tools required for these procedures:

1	_____	4	_____
2	_____	5	_____
3	_____	6	_____

List all supplies required to perform these procedures by interval:

1	_____	4	_____
2	_____	5	_____
3	_____	6	_____

Equipment
Running
Y or N ?   Procedure:

Bimonthly PM Procedure

List all special tools required for these procedures:

1 _____   4 _____
2 _____   5 _____
3 _____   6 _____

List all supplies required to perform these procedures by interval:

1 _____   4 _____
2 _____   5 _____
3 _____   6 _____

Equipment
Running
Y or N ?   Procedure:

Quarterly PM Procedure

List all special tools required for these procedures:

1 _____   4 _____
2 _____   5 _____
3 _____   6 _____

List all supplies required to perform these procedures by interval:

1 _____   4 _____
2 _____   5 _____
3 _____   6 _____

Equipment
Running
 Y or N ?   Procedure:

Semiannual PM Procedure

List all special tools required for these procedures:

1 _____ 4 _____
2 _____ 5 _____
3 _____ 6 _____

List all supplies required to perform these procedures by interval:

1 _____ 4 _____
2 _____ 5 _____
3 _____ 6 _____

Equipment
Running
 Y or N ?   Procedure:

Annual PM Procedure

List all special tools required for these procedures:

1   ————————————   4   ————————————
2   ————————————   5   ————————————
3   ————————————   6   ————————————

List all supplies required to perform these procedures by interval:

1   ————————————   4   ————————————
2   ————————————   5   ————————————
3   ————————————   6   ————————————

Equipment
Running
  Y or N ?   Procedure:

APPENDIX 4
BLANK FORMS

If you don't currently have workorders, then this appendix compiles examples for your use. To create a professional-looking form, have a printer create a two-part carbonless version. With a two-part form, you get the original and the original author of the PM can also keep a copy of the workorder.

The following forms are offered in this order:

Work Performed Without a Workorder

Workorder, 8 1/2 × 11 Basic

Workorder, 8 1/2 × 11 Coordination

Workorder, 8 1/2 × 11 Drawing

Workorder, 4 × 8 Size (Short Form)

Troubleshooting Guide Form

PM Quality Assurance Form

Parts Requisition Form, 8 1/2 × 11 Size

Parts Requisition Form, 4 × 8 Size (Short Form)

Daily Shift Log

Action Plan

WORK PERFORMED WITHOUT A WORKORDER

BE SURE YOU RECORD DOWNTIME FOR MACHINE

TECHNICIAN:_____ EMP #_____.

DEPT#_____

EQPT#_____

LABOR HRS_____

MACH DOWNTIME_____

DATE_____

EQUIPMENT DESCRIPTION:_____

PROBLEM:_____

_____

ACTION:_____

_____

_____

BE SURE YOU RECORD DOWNTIME FOR MACHINE

TECHNICIAN:_____ EMP #_____.

DEPT#_____

EQPT#_____

LABOR HRS_____

MACH DOWNTIME_____

DATE_____

EQUIPMENT DESCRIPTION:_____

PROBLEM:_____

_____

ACTION:_____

_____

_____

BE SURE YOU RECORD DOWNTIME FOR MACHINE

TECHNICIAN:_____ EMP #_____.

DEPT#_____

EQPT#_____

LABOR HRS_____

MACH DOWNTIME_____

DATE_____

EQUIPMENT DESCRIPTION:_____

PROBLEM:_____

_____

ACTION:_____

_____

_____

BE SURE YOU RECORD DOWNTIME FOR MACHINE

TECHNICIAN:_____ EMP #_____.

DEPT#_____

EQPT#_____

LABOR HRS_____

MACH DOWNTIME_____

DATE_____

EQUIPMENT DESCRIPTION:_____

PROBLEM:_____

_____

ACTION:_____

_____

_____

Work Request (Basic)

Put Your Company Logo Here	Priority: (Check One)

Priority: (Check One)
_____ Safety
_____ High Priority Downtime
_____ Normal Maintenance
_____ Project

Request No:	Cost Center:		Date:
Equipment Number:		Equipment Name:	
Originator:		Need Date:	

Work Requested (include additional sheets or drawings if required):

Action Taken:	Technician:	Date:	Hours:

Parts Used:

Part Number:	Part Name:		Part Number:	Part Name:

Work Accepted: _____   Date: _____

Work Request (Coordination)

	Priority: (Check One)
Put Your Company Logo Here	_____ Safety
	_____ High Priority Downtime
	_____ Normal Maintenance
	_____ Project

Request No:	Cost Center:		Date:

Equipment Number:	Equipment Name:
Originator:	Need Date:

Coordination Signatures:	Date:

Work Requested (include additional sheets or drawings if required):

Action Taken:	Technician:	Date:	Hours:

Parts Used:

Work Accepted: _____   Date: _____

Work Request (Drawing)

Put Your Company Logo Here	**Priority: (Check One)** _____ Safety _____ High Priority Downtime _____ Normal Maintenance _____ Project

Request No:	Cost Center:		Date:

Equipment Number:	Equipment Name:
Originator:	Need Date:

Coordination Signatures:	Date:

Work Requested (include additional sheets):

Include Drawing (If Appropriate)

Action Taken:	Technician:	Date:	Hours:

Parts Used:

Work Accepted: _____   Date: _____

Work Request (Short Form)

Date:

Priority: (Check One)

Safety _____ Normal Maintenance

High Priority Downtime _____ Project

Cost Center:

Request No: Date:

Equipment Number: **Equipment Name:**

Originator: **Need Date:**

Work Requested (include additional sheets or drawings if required):

Action Taken: | Technician: Date: Hours:

Work Accepted: Date:

Troubleshooting Guide for _____

(As of _____)

Potential Problem or Symptom	Potential Causes	Corrective Actions	Parts

**Preventive Maintenance Quality
Assurance Review**

Date: _____

Technician Reviewed: _____   Reviewer: _____
        Clock No: _____

PM Workorder Reviewed: _____

Workorder   Equipment
    No:_____   Interval: _____   No:_____

Time Work   Time Work
    Started:_____   Completed: _____

Workorder Quality:	Circle one:	
Were all safety procedures followed?	Y	N
Did technician have all required tools?	Y	N
Did workorder provide sufficient information?		
logic flow?	Y	N
required parts?	Y	N
timing and alignment?	Y	N

Please provide additional information on all NO answers and recommended changes:

_____
_____
_____
_____
_____

Technician Performance:	Circle one:	
Demonstrated understanding of safety requirements?	Y	N
Demonstrated understanding of procedure?	Y	N
Any additional training required?	Y	N
Cleaned area upon completion of work?	Y	N

Please provide additional information on all NO answers and required training or improvements:

_____
_____
_____
_____
_____

Parts Requisition Form

Requester: _____   Date: _____

Equipment Number
or
Workorder Number: _____   Need Date: _____

Cost Center: _____

Part No:	Description:	Vendor	Qty:

**Reason
Required:** _____

_____

_____

_____

_____

_____

Approvals: _____

_____   _____
Date

_____   _____
Date

Is this an Emergency: **Yes:** _____   **No:** _____

Safety: _____

Production: _____

Parts Requisition Form (Short Form)

Requester: _____ Date: _____

Equipment Number _____

or

Workorder Number: _____

Need Date: _____

Part No:	Description:	Vendor	Qty:

Reason Required: _____

Approvals: _____ Date

_____ Date

DAILY SHIFT LOG

WO #	WO DESCRIPTION	Estimated Time		Shift	Date	Total Hrs Available / Total Call Hrs	Areas Cleaned:	Maint. Shop	Welding Area	Tech Room	Manuals	Parts Bench	COMMENTS
	COMPRESSOR CHECK												

Action Plan:

Start Date: _____

Champion: _____

Action Steps	Who	Weeks	1	2	3	4	5	6	7	8	9	10	11	12	13	14	15	16	17	18	19	20	% Complete
																							20 40 60 80 100

APPENDIX 5
TEST TIME ANSWERS

This appendix contains suggested answers to the Test Time questions at the end of Chapters 3, 4, 5, and 8. As with most questions associated with facilities management, seldom is there one absolute answer. The answers here represent how I would address these various problem situations, based on my years of experience and training.

CHAPTER 3

1   Based on the plant layout in Figure 3-7, there are two possible ways to define the "logical parts" of the plant:
   ◆ A five-part structure based on the plant's product lines, as follows:
   Raw material area
   Product A area
   Product B area

Office and common areas
Warehouse and shipping areas
◆ A six-part structure based on the following process operations:
Raw materials
Stamping
Grinding
Finishing
Office
Warehouse and shipping

2 A wall between Product A and Product B production equipment would lead you to favor the five-part structure based on the product lines (see Figure A5-1). Alternatively, if the wall were placed between the grinding and finishing areas, then you might favor the structure based on process operations. In addition, with a wall between grinding and finishing, you could combine stamping and grinding operations into one group. (Once again, no one right answer exists—look at your plant and make the decision based on what works best for you.)

CHAPTER 4

1 The equipment numbers required for the office and warehouse/shipping areas will be covered in Appendix 2 in the building equipment lists 1XX and 2XX. The raw material area may be covered by the 1XX and 2XX lists in Appendix 2 as well, but may require its own section. Therefore, I suggest the following assignments (shown pictorially in Figure A5-2):

Figure A5-1. Plant with walls added.

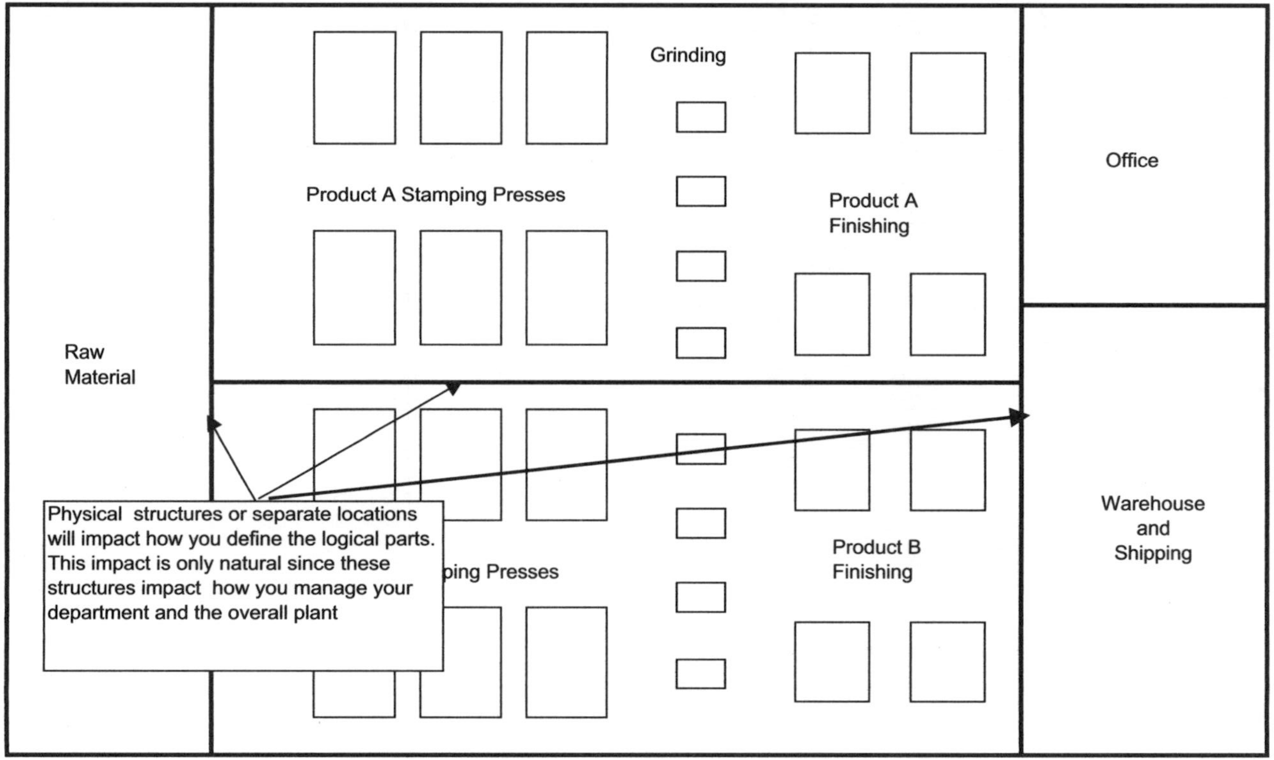

Office

Warehouse
and
Shipping

Product A
Finishing

Product B
Finishing

Grinding

Product A Stamping Presses

ping Presses

Raw
Material

Physical structures or separate locations
will impact how you define the logical parts.
This impact is only natural since these
structures impact how you manage your
department and the overall plant

Figure A5-2. Assignment of three-digit equipment number prefixes for a typical plant.

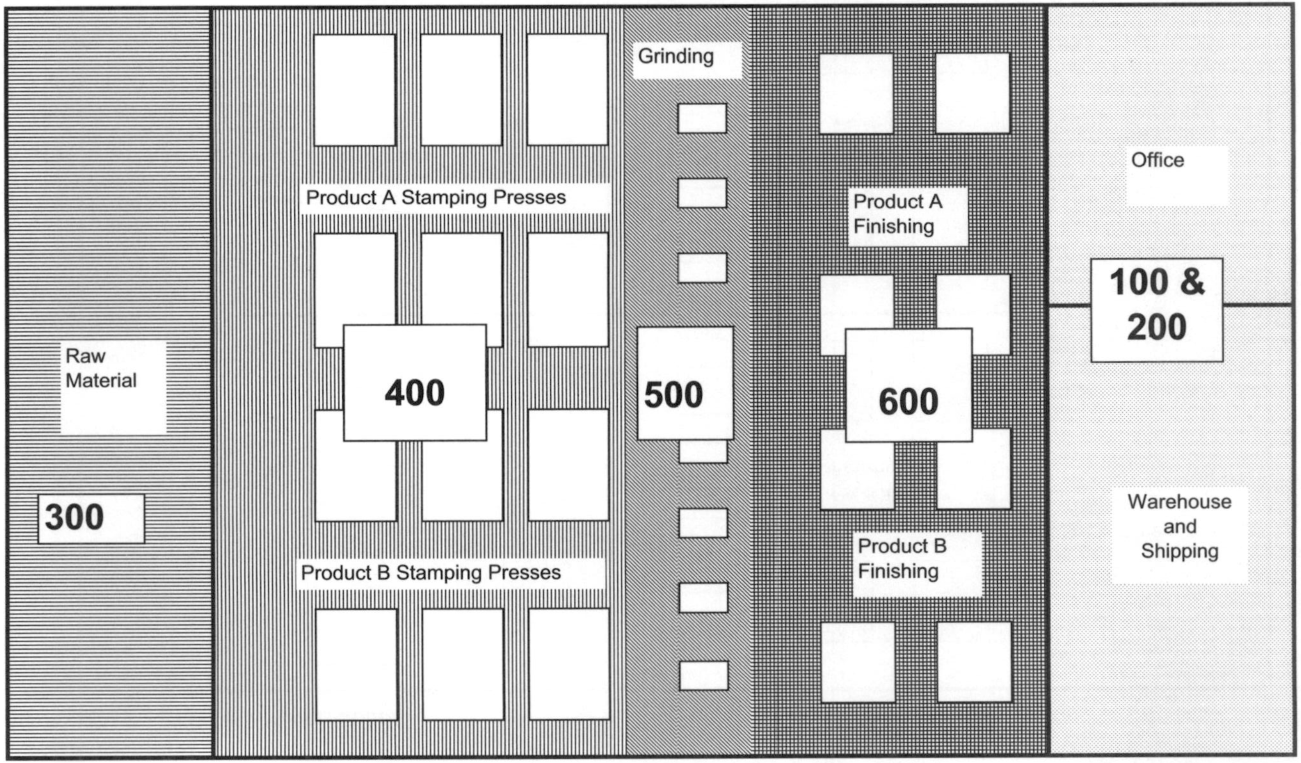

300   Raw Material Handling Equipment
400   Stamping Equipment
500   Grinding Equipment
600   Finishing Equipment

2   I would not assign the pumps their own equipment numbers. The pumps sit on the same pallet as the cooling tower reservoir tank and should be managed as part of the larger system. The pallet has one control panel that controls all pumping activity.

3   The ladder should have its own equipment number. Ladders should be considered safety equipment and inspected monthly for condition. (The monthly inspection helps keep track of those expensive fiberglass ladders.)

CHAPTER 5

1   Each of the three "definitive steps" is notable for the following reasons:

   a. Though the first instruction makes good use of action words and the required grease (i.e., high temp) is specified, the number of lubrication points is not spelled out.

   b. This instruction is a semiannual task hiding in a monthly PM workorder.

   c. The third example is fine. The instruction, as written, uses an action word and specifies the amount and type of oil to use.

2. While the basic structure of the PM workorder is okay, plenty of room exists for improvement. The

PM fails to include important details. Dissecting the instructions as written, step by step, I'd suggest these changes:

◆ The PM should list the gage reading (e.g., 1.2, 1.5) that should trigger the filter change.

◆ The instruction "Verify fan motor is off" is a major no-no. This instruction should direct the technician to lockout the fan motor.

◆ The PM should list the size, type, and quantity of filters required to complete the changeout.

◆ The PM should instruct the technician to re-move the lockout and restart the fan at the end of the job.

A potential rewrite of this PM workorder might look like this:

Air Filter Inspection and Filter Change

_____ Check Air Handler Magnahelic gage and change filter if reading exceeds 1.25.

_____ If a filter change is required, then turn Air Han-dler MCC-04 controls to "off" position and lockout fan motor.

_____ Replace all filters. A complete change will re-quire six 15″ × 20″ × 2″ pleated air filters.

_____ Remove lockout and return MCC-04 to "Auto-matic" position.

CHAPTER 8

1 Each of the three scenarios (a, b, and c) leads you down a potentially different solution path. There-

fore you must collect data and ask questions before jumping into correction action.

a. *Failures occur on only one line.* Do a trouble-shooting analysis of the equipment, operating conditions, and operating parameters by asking the following questions:

◆ Are the belts on this line different from the other lines?

◆ Have these machines had any special repairs or overhauls done recently? Or is the converse true—have the other machines had overhauls?

◆ Are the PM schedules up to date?

◆ When the belts fail, are the failures all the same?

◆ Does this line run faster than the other lines?

◆ Are the parts produced on this line unique from the other lines?

◆ Are the operating parameters different for this line compared with the other lines?

◆ How does the experience of the operators compare between lines?

◆ How does this line's scheduled runtime compare to the scheduled runtime for the other lines?

b. *First pull machine belts fail on each line.* In this case, consider these questions:

◆ Are all the belt failures similar?

◆ Are there differences between the PM workorders for the first and second pull machines?

◆ Do the operating conditions vary on a line

from the first machine to the second machine?

◆ On a line, does one person operate both machines, or do different (and separate) people operate the machine?

◆ Does operation of the machines rotate among a pool of operators?

c. *Belts fail randomly.* In this final scenario, consider these questions:

◆ Are all the belt failures similar?

◆ Have all the machines been maintained with the same spare parts?

◆ Do the belt failures follow (or proceed) any special maintenance activities?

◆ Do these failures occur while running particular parts or parts with common characteristics?

◆ Do the failures occur on any particular day or shift?

2 To determine why one of the electrical panels trips out during the summer and winter but not in the spring and fall, I would begin by asking these questions:

a. Does the panel that trips have any mechanical issues—loose wires, lugs, or busbars, etc.?

b. What is the electrical load for the panel that trips?

◆ Is it at rated capacity or near rated capacity?

◆ Does the panel have cyclic-type loads like air conditioners and furnaces?

◆ What type of routine load variation does this panel experience?

c. How does the electrical load on this panel

compare (in terms of type and variation) to the load on the panel that does not trip?

Chapter 8's Test Time questions illustrate a simple fact: Until you collect the data and answer the right questions, you will not know what direction to take to resolve failures. Welcome to the real world of maintenance!

APPENDIX 6
MANAGING THE SYSTEM
WITHOUT A COMPUTERIZED
PM PROGRAM

Although I highly recommend the purchase of a computerized PM program, I realize that not everyone needs or desires to purchase a program. I have developed this appendix to allow you to implement and manage your PM program without a computerized maintenance management system (CMMS).

Without a CMMS, you essentially need to duplicate its functions—creating PM workorders, scheduling PM workorders, and collecting historical equipment data—manually. This system will resemble the card systems of yesterday. The process requires the following steps:

1   Type up the PM workorders created by following the process described in Chapter 5.

2   Set up a file system to schedule the workorders and to maintain the equipment history.

3　Copy the appropriate number of PM workorders and place them in the appropriate file system.

4　File the completed workorders in historical files.

TYPE UP THE PM WORKORDERS

Type up the workorders using a word processing program. This step creates files for future updating. Once you have these workorders created, then print them for filing in step 3. Treat these newly printed PM workorders as a master copy of all the PMs.

SET UP THE FILES

You will require a filing system to hold the PM workorders and another set of files to store the completed PM workorders. The scheduling files will consist of a file created for each week of the year.

These files will hold all the workorders scheduled to be completed during that week. The historical file will consist of a file for each piece of equipment. Use the equipment list developed in Chapter 4 to assemble the files.

MAKE COPIES OF THE PM WORKORDERS AND FILES

Take the master copy of the PM workorders and make the appropriate number of copies of each workorder required for the entire year. For example, a weekly PM workorder on a mixer would require fifty-two copies, or one for each week.

Now take these workorders and place them in the appropriate weekly files. For example, the weekly PM workorders on our mixer would be placed in each of the weekly files. For PM workorders with intervals greater than one week, follow the scheduling suggestions in Chapter 6. Once you have the files set up, you pull the files weekly and schedule the PM workorders using the process setup in Chapter 2.

FILE THE COMPLETED PM WORKORDERS

When the completed workorders are returned in the daily files, then file the workorders in their historical equipment file. This step allows you to collect historical equipment data and to document program compliance for auditors.

SUMMARY

Follow the four steps outlined to implement the program described in this book. Make sure to keep the PM workorders created in step 1 as a master copy. Use this master copy as the basis for making copies to file in the weekly files. File completed workorders in a historical file to develop equipment history.

Implementation of the four steps sounds easy and straightforward, and in fact, it is an easy system to manage in a small facility. However, in a larger plant, you will be overwhelmed by the administration a manual system requires. Trend data will be especially cumbersome to develop and track.

If you decide not to purchase a computerized PM program, then monitor the workload associated with maintaining the system by hand. If it becomes evident that you need a computerized program, then the structure and workorders you have already set up should readily transfer to the computerized program.

APPENDIX 7
SUMMARY OF HELPFUL TIPS

This appendix lists all the Helpful Tips suggested in the body of the book. I have added this appendix so that as you start to implement your PM program, you will avoid the frustration of flipping through the book looking for that one tip you want to review but don't remember where you saw it. You can go back to the chapters for more details behind the topics, if necessary. Use Appendix 4 to obtain some blank forms to use.

CHAPTER 2: GETTING STARTED

Helpful Tip 1. If you get a workorder you do not know how to complete (but it sounds like a good idea), then schedule it as a two-part workorder:

Part 1 Planning and research

Part 2 Execution

This technique keeps the workorders moving and does not make you personally responsible for developing every repair solution. This approach also starts the empowerment process by forcing your mechanics to start thinking about how to fix the plant's problems.

Helpful Tip 2. Set up a two-week scheduling board that allows you to plan where and when you perform the workorders. The board is a visual management tool to use in planning your daily and weekly schedule. To set up the scheduling board:

◆ Buy a "dry erase board" from a local office supply store.

◆ Buy pinstriping from a local auto supply store.

◆ Mark off grids for each shift (over a fourteen-day period) using the pinstripes.

The schedule board allows you to work through "what-if" situations because you can move the workorders around on the board and see what happens to the schedule if the work is moved up a day or two or pushed back a week. Then, once you have decided on the schedule, you have a visual record of the plan for your review. The completed board will also help in dealing with all those people who want to know when their workorder is scheduled. (Refer to Chapter 2, Figure 2-4, for a picture of a typical scheduling board.)

Helpful Tip 3. If you experience a large percentage of troublecalls, assign specific technicians on a rotating basis to respond to them. Give the float technician small, low-priority workorders to complete between calls. This tactic lets you keep fighting the fires and still get some PM and project workorders done.

Use the Work Performed Without a Workorder form to keep track of the troublecalls. Technicians fill out one of the blocks on this form when they respond to a troublecall. Someone then enters these forms into your CMMS program as completed workorders. The form's format can be tailored so that it's compatible with your CMMS workorder entry screen. Figure 2-5 explains how to fill out the form; a blank form you can copy is available in Appendix 4.

Helpful Tip 4. Set up workorder bins to hold parts for scheduled workorders. Number the bins and write the appropriate bin number on the scheduled workorder. By putting parts in the bins, you eliminate the need for technicians to hunt for the parts they need to complete a workorder. The bins help you keep track of incoming project or repair parts and you create a place to store parts required for ongoing long-term projects.

Helpful Tip 5. Create a filing system for workorders placed on hold while awaiting parts. This "system" can be as simple as a clipboard with the workorders and copies of the purchase orders stapled together. The workorder comes off the clipboard when you receive the parts and they have been placed in a workorder bin.

Helpful Tip 6. Allow your technicians to identify the required parts and fill out the purchase requests for your review and approval. That way you don't become a bottleneck and your technicians improve their knowledge.

Helpful Tip 7. Cross-reference your workorders and purchase requests to reduce confusion. Cross-referencing ensures that incoming parts get used for their original purpose. When a part arrives, the workorder number is right in front of you on the purchase order, so you can use the information on the shipping receipt to identify the intended use of the part.

The cross-referencing process works like this:

◆ Write the workorder number on the purchase request.

◆ Write the purchase request number on the workorder.

◆ Have the workorder number listed on the address header of the shipping receipt.

◆ Place the workorder in the filing system you created and wait for the part to arrive.

Helpful Tip 8. Forward-schedule the weekend (or plant shutdown) workorders. To forward-schedule, put workorders that require downtime in the day shift folder of the next nonwork day (e.g., Saturday, Christmas, etc.). By forward-scheduling, you can forecast the workload for these days. Additionally, you get the workorders off your desk and into a place where they will not be lost. As the holiday or nonwork occasion approaches, pull the file and schedule the workorders.

Helpful Tip 9. Develop a summary sheet to track the scheduled workorders for each shift. On this sheet, list the scheduled workorders and the names of the technicians scheduled for that shift. Place this sheet in each schedule folder once you complete the schedule. If you review this sheet on the following day, you'll know at a glance what you scheduled versus what really happened. You'll also know if a workorder does not come back. Figure 2-6 explains how to fill out the daily shift log; a blank version of this form is available in Appendix 4 for you to copy and use in your operation.

Also, never let technicians hold onto workorders. By requiring technicians to return all workorders to the schedule folder at the end of the shift, you prevent lost workorders and you can track the shift's accomplishments.

Helpful Tip 10. Coordinate your schedule with the production scheduler, supervisor, or manager to make sure your plan does not conflict with their plan. In the best-case scenario, you can develop a schedule that meets both of your needs. In the worst-case scenario, you will avoid the frustration (and possible pain) of having production short-circuit your perfectly planned schedule.

Helpful Tip 11. If deciding on prioritization becomes a nerve-racking experience, then use a prioritization system, ranking tasks by long-term importance and short-range urgency. To use this method (proposed by Alec Mackenzie in his book *The Time Trap*), look at each task and give the task a rank (e.g., 1–3) for importance and urgency. Add up both scores and then schedule the lowest numbers. The exception: Do all the safety hazard workorders immediately.

Helpful Tip 12. When reviewing potential CMMS programs, ask the vendor how the program handles opening and closing workorders. A cumbersome process can tie up administrative time in trying to manage the workorders. A cumbersome system can also prevent you from using the full power of the program—if it's difficult to use, you may eventually stop entering the workorders until they are complete. When choosing a CMMS program:

◆ Be sensitive to the number of screens needed to open and close workorders.

◆ Check if the program allows you to close the workorders from a single menu screen.

CHAPTER 4: DEVELOPING AN EQUIPMENT LIST

Helpful Tip 1. If selecting a sequence becomes an issue, then list all the main categories of equipment and assign the numbers by alphabetical order (e.g., 300—Extrusion, 400—Packaging, 500—Raw Material, and so on).

Helpful Tip 2. Don't fall into the trap of thinking that each process line needs its own three-digit number for each piece of equipment. Develop the three-digit numbers based on the equipment's function rather than make or model.

Helpful Tip 3. If you have more than six process areas, then add a digit to the type category. Under these conditions, the equipment number changes from XXX-XXXX to **X**XXX-XXXX. However, before taking this step, analyze whether you truly have more than six process areas or whether you have failed to properly categorize types.

Helpful Tip 4. Assigning the same technicians to develop the initial list for an entire area will keep the list uniform (rightly or wrongly).

Helpful Tip 5. Use the process of developing an equipment list as an opportunity to bring people on board with the program or kick them off the train. You want to make sure you have a complete list, but give the people making the list some leeway and don't be too critical.

Helpful Tip 6. Don't be too quick to delete those safety items that require periodic inspections—for example, ladders, safety harnesses, and pressure relief valves.

Having these items numbered not only helps to ensure these inspections get done through the issuance of PM workorders, but also allows you to generate a workorder history for the safety and insurance inspectors.

Helpful Tip 7. Let the production folks take a look at the list. Not only does this help to get them on board, but it also allows you to verify that maintenance and production share the same view of the building. (They may even have a few good ideas!)

Helpful Tip 8. The first time you number the plant's equipment, number all the like equipment pieces sequentially as they "sit" in the plant. Sequential numbering makes it easier for the technicians when they start using the PM workorders. After the first pass, you will not be able to follow this sequential process, but by then you will have seasoned people. The difference in numbers will also serve to identify the newer pieces of equipment.

Helpful Tip 9. If you plan to have special tags made for your equipment, initially use duct tape to get the numbers on the equipment. There will be an inevitable delay with the first order of tags. It usually takes time to get the style and format correct. It also takes time for a vendor to produce a large quantity of special tags. Do not add confusion to the PM program implementation by waiting for everything to be perfect before putting numbers on the equipment.

If you decide to have special tags made, then make sure you are happy with the final design before placing the final order or giving production the go-ahead. Do not be afraid to see a production quality draft of the tags. (With the price of these little puppies, you do not want to receive 200 to 300 tags with the wrong format, wrong logo, etc.)

Helpful Tip 10. Avoid using paper or vinyl labels. They do not hold up in the typical plant environment and the writing eventually fades.

Helpful Tip 11. Before ordering tags, discuss your plans with the plant controller, who may want the company's capital equipment number included on each tag. Including this number on the tag may simplify the company's required periodic capital equipment audits.

◆ Do not, however, allow the accountants to talk you into using their number in place of your number since they may have no idea of what you are trying to accomplish through professional maintenance management.

CHAPTER 5: WRITING PMs

Helpful Tip 1. If you have limited resources or you truly have no identical equipment, then pick the piece of equipment or the process line with the greatest amount of downtime. When you finish writing PMs for this piece of equipment or process line, then start on the next piece of equipment or process line with the greatest amount of downtime, and so on and so on.

Helpful Tip 2. If you want to choose a person who cannot write, or does so poorly, then help this person by doing the writing for him or her (either yourself or a supervisor).

Ghostwriting should be done with courtesy, respect, and *confidentiality.*

Helpful Tip 3. Consider tapping your insurance company as a resource for advice on building PM workorders. Insurance companies usually have guidelines for checking sprinkler systems, ventilation systems, boilers, and general safety equipment.

Helpful Tip 4. When you write a PM workorder, put blank lines in front of each step so the technician can check off each step as completed. Checkmarks will indicate whether the technician followed the steps as listed. They also serve as a memory jogger if the technician gets called away before completing the workorder.

Helpful Tip 5. Avoid getting bogged down when trying to get all the settings, measurements, and part numbers for the workorders. Leave a blank on the workorder for the missing data (e.g., "Replace with _____ photoeye") and have the technicians fill in the blanks when they perform the work for the first time.

Helpful Tip 6. As time passes, you may want to change or add information on the workorders. Use Helpful Tip 5 to gather the necessary values and readings by writing a note on the workorder with your request for more information.

Helpful Tip 7. Since writing all the PM workorders will take some time, consider making a master list of all the PM writing workorders so you can track your progress. Use this list as a management tool to make sure you get the workorders done and that you don't forget any pieces of equipment. Figure 5-2 shows a simple format you can use; the list should include the:

◆ Name of the equipment group

◆ Workorder number

◆ Date scheduled

◆ Percentage of work completed

◆ Date completed

CHAPTER 6: DEVELOPING EQUIPMENT MANUALS

Helpful Tip 1. Cut down on your troubleshooting time by:

◆ Placing equipment documentation in your control panels.

◆ Laminating copies of electrical schematics and posting them on the inside of the machine's electrical door panel.

◆ Copying drawings of the PLC I/O modules and coloring in the I/O lights that should be lit for various operations. Laminate these pictures and post them next to the electrical schematics in the control panel.

Helpful Tip 2. To help in the machine lockout process and to improve compliance, post the lockout instructions for each machine on the door of each machine's control panel as well. This action not only simplifies the lockout process, but also raises safety awareness.

And be sure to add an instruction to all monthly equipment PM workorders to verify that lockout instructions are posted on each machine.

Helpful Tip 3. Create a master list of all the workorders related to the creation of your manuals. Use this list to track status and to make sure the work gets done. Use a format similar to the one proposed in Chapter 5 that you used to track your progress in writing PM workorders.

Helpful Tip 4. Put all the manuals in the same color binders and store them by equipment number in a central library. The matching binders give the manuals a professional appearance that goes along with your new approach to maintenance. The standardized colors also make inventorying the manuals and spotting them on the floor easier.

Helpful Tip 5. While you're creating the manuals, verify that you also have backup copies of all computer programs.

Helpful Tip 6. Consider using employees on restricted duty to develop the manuals. Talk to your human resources department about this option—you may help them out while getting the extra help you need. If you follow this tip, then be selective about whom you accept for the project. Also, have some example manuals for them to use as a guide.

Helpful Tip 7. On future equipment purchases, request a troubleshooting guide and recommended PM instructions as part of the purchase. By requesting the guide and the PM list, you reduce the amount of work required to create the new manuals. This information will also help speed up getting the new equipment into production.

Be advised that this special purchase request may not apply to off-the-shelf hardware. However, with the increased focus on ISO standards, many equipment manufacturers have improved their manuals by adding PM recommendations and troubleshooting information

Helpful Tip 8. Use the new troubleshooting guides to review the existing PM workorders and make changes as appropriate. While developing the troubleshooting guide you'll gain new insights into potential failures, which allow you to create better PMs and to identify required spare parts.

Helpful Tip 9. Set up a special work area for manual creation. It doesn't need to be an office or conference room. The area just needs to be a space where the different manual pieces can be spread out and worked on, and where work-in-progress manuals can be left out between workdays. It becomes a lot easier for supervisors and team leaders to keep track of their "manual creators" if they are given a special area in which to work.

CHAPTER 7: SETTING UP INVENTORY

Helpful Tip 1. Before you start wholesale disposal of obsolete parts, check if any other plants in your company need those items. Also check if these parts have any resale value on the open market. Remember, one person's junk is another person's treasure!

Helpful Tip 2. If you want to manage the inventory with a computerized maintenance system, then you will need to have a numbering system. The computer program will have its own numbering system structure and it will require you to develop your inventory numbering system within these constraints. Be flexible and tailor your numbering system to handle certain realities:

◆ Mechanical parts (e.g., gears, bearings, seals) will be numbered different from your electrical components (e.g., photoeyes, proximity switches).

◆ Although every vendor has the "same" 6205 bearing, not all vendors have the same retroreflective photoeye—there may be a different mounting base, polarity, cabling connectors, etc.

Helpful Tip 3. If available floor space is limited, consider installing a mezzanine to expand your parts storage area—but make sure you have sufficient building height and something like twenty-four-foot ceilings to accommodate a mezzanine.

Helpful Tip 4. Consider segregated metal drawers for your fastener storage. The drawers are an efficient way of keeping the nuts, bolts, and screws separated while making resupply simpler. Make sure you put labels on the front of each drawer to reduce search time. Also, segregate fastener types into sections and sort by size within these sections.

Helpful Tip 5. If any of the vendors cannot readily give you information about your purchases for the past year, then you need to determine if you are using the right vendor! My advice, unless they are the only source within 500 miles, change vendors immediately. Don't be confused or misguided—those homegrown, garage-size parts houses cost you money in downtime, expedited freight charges, and higher parts costs.

Helpful Tip 6. If your vendors don't have a large history on your plant, ask them to perform an equipment survey. This survey will match your repair part requirements to the products they sell. With this information, you can make decisions on what you need to stock because you will have data on the quantity such as parts you have in the operation.

◆ When *you request* a vendor to perform a survey, there are expectations of future orders. Be ethical and use this tip appropriately.

On the flip side, many vendors will offer to perform the survey as a way to generate future business. In this situation, you are not under any implied obligation to buy!

Helpful Tip 7. To simplify your structure, identify everyday-use items (e.g., nuts, bolts, gloves, caulk) and treat them as expendables. Set them up in easy-access cabinets, with the reorder list posted on the door, and use a kanban system to maintain the stocking levels. In addition:

◆ If you have a large enough list of expendables, consider sourcing all these items to one vendor and having this vendor maintain the stock for you.

◆ If you do not have a large enough expendables list, then you can still source these items, except you will have to maintain the stock. Work with the vendor to set up a standard reorder list that you can fill in and fax to the vendor.

◆ Check with your purchasing people, you may find that setting up a sole source for expendable items is an excellent opportunity to establish a prototype electronic ordering project with a major MRO supplier. Then your personnel can use barcode labels and handheld scanners to create replenishment orders for expendable supplies.

Helpful Tip 8. While deciding how you want to maintain your parts, look at the available management reports from your computerized maintenance management system. These reports may give you ideas on how to manage the inventory once you know what is available for use. This review will also help you identify which fields *must* be completed to effectively manage parts with your software program.

Helpful Tip 9. If you are using a manual system of index cards to maintain your inventory, have the cards preprinted with the desired information. The preprinted card not only looks professional, but also standardizes the way the information is gathered and maintained. A two-sided card can fit information pertaining to:

◆ Part number

◆ Name of primary vendor and phone number

◆ Name of alternative vendor and phone number

◆ Price

◆ Maximum and minimum quantities

◆ Reorder history (i.e., quantities ordered and their dates)

Helpful Tip 10. Always keep a backup copy of the information recorded on your inventory index cards because these little cards have been known to sprout wings!

Helpful Tip 11. If you have items that you repair and replace in the inventory, then create a "repair warehouse." The repair warehouse allows you to return the item to storage, but does not artificially inflate the carrying cost of your inventory. You only need the repair warehouse if you have a computerized inventory that automatically assigns value to each item received into the inventory. The repair warehouse allows you to repair parts while keeping the accountants (who are watching the value of the inventory) happy.

Chapter 8: Maintaining the System

Helpful Tip 1. Start an "Open Workorder Report" to keep people informed of the status of their workorder. This report does not need to be elaborate; at minimum include the workorder number, name of the requester, date of origination, topic, and comments. Send the list out weekly and you will eliminate calls about workorders.

◆ *Cautionary Note:* Once you start sending this report out, then you definitely need to keep moving the workorders through the system. If you do not manage the workorders, then everybody knows because you told them in the report!

Helpful Tip 2. If you purchase a computerized maintenance management program, then make sure it can generate the Open Workorder Report as part of its "canned" management reports. If the program has the report already set up, then you can automatically generate the report weekly and send it out.

Helpful Tip 3. Make the basic workorder form a two-part form so the originator can keep the copy for their records. If you lose someone's workorder, then you can get a copy from them. If you stay on top of your workorders, the two-part form can be a useful tool for communicating with people in your company—but it can also be used as a powerful weapon against you if you do not manage the workorders!

Helpful Tip 4. As you embark on the path of continuous improvement, look for ways to improve the repair time for equipment. Specifically:

◆ Look for areas where quick disconnects or bypasses make sense and will help in repairs. Adding valves and quick connects can be an expensive proposition, so use these items where a potential payback exist.

◆ When you make such changes, make sure that the plugs, valves, or connectors are properly sized and allowed by the applicable building code.

◆ Be sure to mark any new valves or bypasses so that technicians and operators know their intended use. Nothing hurts your credibility more than to incur downtime or process scrap because someone closed or opened the wrong valve.

Helpful Tip 5. To spot trends, set up separate semi-annual or annual reviews with your three or four largest suppliers. During this review, look at the top five to ten items you purchase most from each vendor. Close this review by challenging your vendors to suggest options for reducing these quantities.

Helpful Tip 6. As you discover trends and look for ways to improve your maintenance program, assess whether the problem area might best be handled by an outside service. For example, many companies outsource HVAC maintenance to ensure compliance with Environmental Protection Agency rules. Other areas where outsourcing might apply include hoist inspections, confined space repairs, fire extinguisher inspections, and sprinkler system inspections. Make your outsourcing decisions based on your department goals, cost considerations, and whether the outside service's quality meets your expectations.

Helpful Tip 7. Use production data to spot trends or identify issues. The scrap and productivity reports should show the equipment-related problems. Remember, though, that nothing undermines your credibility more than well intentioned but unguided continuous improvement projects. Therefore:

◆ Do not take the raw data on face value. You must ask questions and understand the data to make sure you are on the right problem/solution track.

◆ Share this information with the people in your department, and ask for their input on why these problems are occurring and what the potential solutions are.

◆ Proceed to solve the problem only after you have the facts and input from your staff.

Helpful Tip 8. If you identify any equipment requiring routine rebuilds, but you find yourself unable to continually apply resources, consider outsourcing the rebuild to a local shop. In this case:

◆ When you send out equipment for rebuild, be selective about who you choose; make sure the service providers have the resources to do the job, and give them any required tips or training.

◆ If you find the rebuild program helps, then evaluate whether you want to bring the work in-house in six to eight months. You can use the cost data for the outside shop to justify/offset the labor cost.

◆ Be sure to monitor your outside vendors to make sure they stick to the agreed schedule and maintain expected quality levels.

Helpful Tip 9. To prevent major building problems, make sure your new PM program includes checks of the electrical panels, roof, and sprinkler system. Consider that:

◆ An annual infrared (IR) scan of all electrical panels can save major repair dollars and downtime.

◆ An annual roof inspection by a trained professional can prevent leaks and deterioration.

◆ A well-maintained sprinkler system has obvious importance.

Helpful Tip 10. To avoid problem startups after major PM overhauls, create a checklist of startup steps and related safety checks. When you create this checklist (or any other form recommended throughout this book), consider numbering the forms to help track their evolution. If you work in a facility that has ISO or QS certification, then this tip is a requirement for document control. In ISO- or QS-certified facilities, work with your local coordinators to make sure you follow the established guidelines for your facility.

CHAPTER 9: PLANNING FOR SUCCESS

Helpful Tip 1. Don't be boxed into thinking that only team members can create equipment lists and PM workorders. If you've passed over some of your best people because you need them to run the plant, you can still have them participate by asking them to review the drafts of the building breakdown, the equipment list, PM workorders, and inventory additions. By engaging your "stars" in this way you are helping to ensure you get their program buy-in.

Helpful Tip 2. Do not forget to plan for administrative support. Someone needs to turn this data into workorders.

Even if you do not have a computerized preventive maintenance program, you will still need to put the information into a typed format. With spare clerical support in short supply in most organizations, consider hiring temporary help to get the information typed up. But save the final decision on administrative resources until you have reviewed the plan with your boss. Your boss may have suggestions for resources that you did not think of or thought were off-limits.

Helpful Tip 3. Don't overlook hourly associates as potential candidates to schedule workorders and order parts. By assigning these positions to hourly associates, you may create a more workable solution for your boss and the human resources department. If you determine you do not have any in-house candidates, then consult HR on options to fill your needs.

Helpful Tip 4. If a scheduled activity lasts longer than one week, then schedule periodic reviews. These reviews should assess schedule status and program workorder status. Use the PM workorder development master list (discussed in Chapter 5) to track progress.

Helpful Tip 5. To keep your project focused, set up an Action Plan schedule in increments of days and weeks.

Figure 9-1 shows a sample schedule with an implementation timeline; a blank Action Plan form you can copy is also available in Appendix 4. This schedule format will also work for other projects.

Helpful Tip 6. Do not develop your plans in a vacuum. Just as you need a team to successfully implement the program, you need your boss's support. To that end:

◆ Discuss your plans to form a team and to implement the seven-step process with your boss before forming the implementation team.

◆ Give your bosses a copy of this book so they understand how you will implement the program.

Helpful Tip 7. Create an information board for sharing the schedule and pertinent information to keep everyone informed of the project's progress. Use this board to post the draft documents such as the equipment lists.

INDEX

abbreviations, commonly used, 153–154
Action Plan (form), 182
administrative support, planning for, 141
Annual PM Procedure Worksheet, 170
authors, PM, 74–75

Bimonthly PM Procedure Worksheet, 167
binders (for manuals), 89–90
bins
    parts, 101, 102
    workorder, 25
blowers, 60
boards, scheduling, 23–24
boss's input, getting, 146, 147
breakdowns, responding to, 6
building equipment, numbering of,
    157–158
building maintenance, 45–47

cabinets, modular, 101–103
card systems (for inventory management),
    111–113, 193
CMMSs, see computerized maintenance
    management systems
complex systems, equipment lists for, 60,
    61
complex workorders, scheduling, 22

computerized maintenance management
    systems (CMMSs), 3, 152, 193–196
and continuous improvement, 134
generating Open Workorder Report
    from, 121–122
for inventory management, 99–101,
    109, 110
low-priority workorders in, 25
for parts inventory, 99
scheduling with, 31
computers, assessing need for, 2–5
continuous improvement, 12, 125–132,
    134
copies (of PM workorders), 194–195
cross-referencing (of workorders and pur-
    chase requests), 27

Daily PM Procedure Worksheet, 163
Daily Shift Log (form), 181
data, adding missing, 79
day, scheduling by, 21–23
details, adding missing, 79
draft PM workorders, 78–80
drawers (for fastener storage), 103, 104

electrical panels, 131
Environmental Protection Agency, 130

219

equipment, 9–10, 51–71
  initial list of, 63
  labels for, 65–67
  master list of, 51–56, 62–65
  numbering system for managing, 56–62,
    65–68, 155–160
  and production staff, 65
  surveys of, 106
  troubleshooting, 127
Every-Other-Week PM Procedure Work-
    sheet, 165
existing stock, sorting/organizing,
    100–103
expendable inventory, 106–108

failure(s)
  avoiding, in scheduling, 23
  learning from, 32, 132–133
fans, 126–128
fastener storage, drawers for, 103, 104
feedback, evaluating, 82
files
  shift, 17, 18, 32
  workorder, 25, 27, 194, 195
floating technicians, 24–26
folders, scheduling, 17–18
forward-scheduling, 27–28, 32

hourly associates, 143
hours, calculating scheduling, 18–20
HVAC systems, 130

implementation, program, 7–12, 143–148
information boards, 148
infrared (IR) scans, 131
instructions, writing good, 76–78
insurance companies, 75
inventory management, 11–12, 97–118
  and adding new parts, 114, 115
  card system for, 111–113
  computerized, 99–101, 109, 110
  elements of, 98
  and equipment surveys, 106
  of expendables, 106–108
  and getting information from vendors,
    105
  and improvement of inventory,
    104–106
  and improvement of uptime, 116–117

mezzanines for, 103
of new inventory, 112
numbering system for, 101
and obsolete parts, 100, 114, 116
and purchases of additional inventory
  items, 108, 109
and reordering plan, 109–111
reports for, 110
segregated metal drawers for, 103, 104
and sorting/organizing of existing stock,
  100–103
steps in, 99–113
inventory stocking form, 115
I/O lights, 86
IR (infrared) scans, 131
ISO-9000, 30
ISO standards, 93

labels, equipment, 65–67
lockout instructions, 86–87
logical parts, defining, 9, 37–50
  and plant vs. building maintenance,
    45–47
  starting process of, 41, 45
long-term resource requirements, planning
  for, 142–143
low-priority workorders, handling, 25

machine lockout instructions, 86–87
Mackenzie, Alec, 29
maintenance of PM systems, 119–138
  and availability of parts, 124–125
  computerized systems for, 121–122, 134
  and continuous improvement, 125–132
  elements of, 119
  and keeping workorders current, 124
  and learning from failures, 132–133
  and purchase reviews, 129
  and quality level, 122–124
  safety guidelines for, 133–134
  and scheduling of workorders, 120–122
  startup checklist for, 133
  using production data in, 130
management, inventory, *see* inventory
  management
manuals, 11, 85–96
  binders for, 89–90
  creating, 87–90, 93–94
  editing, 94

elements of, 85
getting material for, 89
maintaining, 94–95
need for, 86
"other significant items" in, 90–91
reviewing, 94
troubleshooting guides in, 91–93
updating, 94
mapping, 9
master equipment list, 51–56, 62–65
creation of, 63–64
structure of, 53–56
master workorder list (for creation of manuals), 89
mezzanines, 103
mind-set, 5–7
missing data, adding, 79
modular cabinets, 101–103
monitoring, 12
Monthly PM Procedure Worksheet, 166
motors, 60

new inventory
adding, 114
maintaining, 112
numbering systems, 10, 54–57, 101, 155–160

obsolete parts, 100
"Open Workorder Reports," 121–122
operating conditions, troubleshooting, 127
operating parameters, troubleshooting, 128
"other significant items" section (in manual), 90–91
outsourcing (maintenance of PM systems), 130, 131

participation, encouraging, 9, 64
parts
adding new, 114, 115
availability of, 124–125
bins for, 101, 102
CMMSs for inventory of, 99
obsolete, 100, 114, 116
Parts Requisition Form(s)
long, 179
short, 180
personal data assistants (PDAs), 4
physical boundaries, 41

planning, 12–13, 139–149
for administrative support, 141
getting your boss's input in, 146, 147
for hourly associates, 143
and identification of implementation steps, 143–148
for long-term resource requirements, 142–143
for reordering, 109–111
for short-term resource requirements, 140–141
use of information board in, 148
see also scheduling
plant maintenance, 45–47
plant structure, 38–44
PM instructions (PM workorders), 6, 10–11, 37, 73–84
authors of, 74–75
components of successful, 76
draft vs. final, 78–80
and quality assurance, 81–83
scheduling, 34–35, 80–81
steps in writing, 76–78
throwing away, 30
PM procedure worksheet(s), 76, 161–170
annual, 170
bimonthly, 167
daily, 163
every-other-week, 165
monthly, 166
quarterly, 168
semiannual, 169
weekly, 164
PM Quality Assurance Review (form), 178
predictive maintenance, 55
prioritizing (of workorders), 19, 21, 25, 29–30
process equipment, numbering of, 159–160
production data, using, 130
production staff
and equipment, 65
scheduling and coordination with, 29
program implementation, 7–12, 143–148
pumps, 60
purchase requests, 27

quality
maintenance of PM systems and level of, 122–124
of PM instructions, 81–83

Quarterly PM Procedure Worksheet, 168

RCM (reliability-centered maintenance), 55
rebuilds, 131
reliability-centered maintenance (RCM), 55
reordering (of inventory), 109–111
repair warehouses, 112, 114
reports
  inventory management, 110
  of open workorders, 121–122
reviews
  of manual, 94
  of purchases, 129
  scheduling of, 144
  of shift files, 32
roofs, 131

safety
  inspecting for, 64
  and maintenance of PM systems, 133–134
scheduling, 8, 9, 15–36
  achieving success with, 23, 31–35
  avoiding failure in, 23, 120–122
  and calculation of available scheduling hours, 18–20
  and completion of workorders, 30–31
  of complicated workorders, 22
  computerized PM programs for, 31
  and coordination with production staff, 29
  and cross-referencing of workorders and purchase requests, 27
  by day and by shift, 21–23
  forward-, 27–28, 32
  of PM workorders, 80–81
  and prioritizing of workorders, 19, 21, 29–30
  of reviews, 144
  sample form for, 145–146
  scope of, 15–16
  setting up shift files for, 17, 18
  summary sheet for, 28–29
  two-week board for, 23–24
  use of filing systems for, 25, 27

  and use of floating technicians, 24–26
  use of workorder bins for, 24–26
  see also planning
Semiannual PM Procedure Worksheet, 169
shift, scheduling by, 21–23
shift files
  reviewing, 32
  setting up, 17, 18
shift summary sheets, 32
short-term resource requirements, planning for, 140–141
sprinkler systems, 131–132
startup checklists, 133
stocking form, inventory, 115
summary sheets, 28–29
surveys, equipment, 106

tags, labeling, 66–67
The Time Trap (Alec Mackenzie), 29–30
total productive maintenance (TPM), 55
total productive work (TPW), 6–7, 16
TPM (total productive maintenance), 55
TPW, *see* total productive work
troublecalls, responding to, 6
troubleshooting
  procedure for, 125–126
  reducing time spent on, 86
troubleshooting guides, 91–93, 177
two-week scheduling boards, 23–24

updates (to manual), 94

vendors, getting inventory information from, 105, 130

Weekly PM Procedure Worksheet, 164
workorder bins, 25
workorders, *see* PM instructions
Work Performed Without a Workorder (form), 25, 26, 172
Work Request(s)
  basic, 173
  coordination, 174
  drawing, 175
  short form, 176
writing workorders, 76–78

About the Author

John M. Gross attended Washington University on a U.S. Air Force ROTC scholarship. Upon graduation with a degree in electrical engineering, he entered the U.S. Air Force as a project manager. After seven years in the military, he entered private industry. In his civilian career he has been a plant engineer, engineering manager, business unit manager, and corporate engineer in both the food and automotive industries.

His writings on the subject of productivity have been published internationally in various trade magazines. He holds a master's of administration degree from Central Michigan University. He is a licensed professional engineer, a Six Sigma Blackbelt, an ASQ Certified Quality Engineer, and an AFE Certified Plant Engineer.

He lives in Washington, Missouri, with his wife and two sons.